Automatic Algorithm Recognition and Replacement
A New Approach to Program Optimization

Robert Metzger and Zhaofang Wen

The MIT Press
Cambridge, Massachusetts
London, England

This book was set in Times Roman by the author using the LaTeX document preparation system.
Printed on recycled paper and bound in the United States of America.

Library of Congress Cataloging-in-Publication Data

Metzger, Robert C. Automatic algorithm recognition and replacement: a new
  approach to program optimization / Robert Metzger, Zhaofang Wen.   p.
  cm.
  Includes bibliographical references and index.
  ISBN 0-262-13386-7 (alk. paper)
  1. Computer algorithms. 2. Computer programming. I. Wen, Zhaofang. II.
  Title.
QA76.9.A43 M48 2000
005.1–dc21
99-088044

Contents

List of Figures

List of Tables

Acknowledgments

This work was partially sponsored by the Air Force Material Command and the Advanced Research Projects Agency / CSTO, under ARPA Order No. B548, issued by ESC/ENS under Contract #F19628-94-C-0058. The remainder of the work was funded by the Convex Division of the Hewlett-Packard Company, formerly Convex Computer Corporation. We thank both ARPA and Convex/HP for allowing us to undertake this project.

Wen would like to express his appreciation to Terry Caracuzzo, Mark Schroeder, and Robert Cox for sharing their valuable in-depth experiences of the Convex optimizing compiler. He also enjoyed many interesting conversations with Terry Caracuzzo on compiler optimizations that not only helped the implementations of our preprocessing transformations, but also sharpened the ideas of the system design. He thanks Derek G. Corneil for pointing out the best algorithms on graph isomorphism. He would also like to thank Stephan Olariu for stimulating discussions on algorithms design and for pointing out references in graph theory related to this project. He is very grateful to C. Mike Overstreet for first introducing him to the field of program analysis and transformation.

Presley Smith and Steve Wallach encouraged Metzger to seek external funding for his research ideas. He thanks them for their support and confidence in his efforts. Randall Mercer wrote the first pattern matching transformations in the Convex vectorizing Fortran compiler, which eventually convinced Metzger of the value of the concept and the impossibility of the approach.

Greg Astfalk and Joel Williamson found numerous mistakes in our first draft and suggested corrections on both form and content. We thank them both for their diligent efforts. Augustin Dubrulle provided the QR triangularization example in the introductory chapter. Sean Stroud and Matthew Diaz helped us resurrect the Convex Application Compiler for use in preprocessing application codes.

We acknowledge the comments of the anonymous referees, which helped us improve the text in several ways, as well as the help of our editor at MIT Press, Doug Sery, who helped us navigate the seemingly interminable path from draft to book.

Any errors that remain are purely the responsibility of the authors.

1 Introduction

1.1 Background

Optimizing compilers have a fundamental problem. No matter how powerful their optimizations are, they are no substitute for good application algorithms. Consider the case of sorting. For sufficiently large data sets, a merge sort algorithm compiled with a less powerful optimizer will always out-perform a selection sort algorithm compiled with the most powerful optimizer. Or consider the case of solving systems of equations. For sufficiently large data sets, a Gaussian Elimination algorithm compiled with a less powerful optimizer will always out-perform a Cramer's rule algorithm compiled with the most powerful optimizer.

Developers of optimizing compilers also have an opportunity to leverage an under-used asset. There are several high-quality numerical libraries that are publicly available, such as the BLAS and LAPACK, that provide broadly applicable algorithms for scientific and engineering computing. Vendors of high performance computers often provide versions of these libraries that have been highly tuned to their particular system architecture. Users of high performance computers sometimes employ these libraries. Unfortunately, many users are unaware of their existence, and don't use them even when they are available.

What if compilers could recognize a poor algorithm written by a user, and replace it with the best implementation of a better algorithm that solves the same problem? Given reasonable implementations of both algorithms, such a replacement would result in as significant performance improvement. This book explains an approach that makes this possible.

The scope over which compilers perform optimizations has steadily increased in the past three decades. Initially, they performed optimizations on a sequence of statements that would be executed as a unit, e.g. a basic block. During the 1970's, researchers developed **control flow analysis**, **data flow analysis** and **name association** algorithms. This made it possible for compilers to do optimizations across an entire procedure. During the 1980's, researchers extended these analyses across procedure boundaries (10), as well as adding **side effect analysis** (9). This made it possible for compilers to do optimizations across an entire program.

We can characterize the analyses behind these optimizations from another perspective besides scope. They all add data structures that represent information synthesized from the program source. Some add new abstract entities, like a basic block. Others add new relationships, like **control flow dominance**. Some add both. The more abstract entities and relationships a compiler has available to characterize the semantics of a program, the more opportunities exist for optimization.

Now that commercial compilers can analyze a program across its entire scope, optimization researchers need to ask where the next layer of synthesized information will come from. This book explains an approach that adds a whole new layer of entities and relationships to the semantic analysis that compilers can perform on application codes.

Parallel computation will be the norm in the twenty-first century. Parallel hardware has gone from use in super-computers to departmental servers. Recently, we have seen multiple processors available even in high-end workstations and PC's. Unfortunately, the parallel potential of hardware has raced far ahead of the parallel applications of software.

There are currently two approaches to applying parallelism to applications. The first is to write completely new applications in new languages. Abandoning applications that work is simply unacceptable to most non-academic users of high performance computers.

The second approach is to convert existing applications written in existing languages to a parallel form. This can be done manually or automatically. The labor required to rewrite applications to make use of current parallel systems is great. Even partial success in automatically parallelizing existing codes has obvious economic advantages. This book explains an approach to automatically parallelizing applications that is complementary to current automatic parallelization methods.

1.2 Research Motivations

The research efforts related to our work can be divided into two groups, according to the motivation of the project. The ultimate purpose of the first group is to display information for a person to look at. The end purpose of the system may simply be to provide some form of documentation to the user. Or, after the display, an intelligent user may direct the system to modify a program source in some way. Having a human agent to operate the system makes it possible to use implementation approaches that do not provide complete analyses or that are not provably correct.

The ultimate purpose of the other group is to replace sections of the program source entirely automatically. The end purpose of the system may be to optimize the performance of the application with respect to some resource. Or, the system may improve some quality of the program, such as numerical precision. In either case, the requirement to perform the transformations automatically makes it impossible to use implementation approaches that do not provide complete and provably correct analyses.

1.3   Informal Introduction to the Problem

Consider the Fortran subroutine displayed in Fig.(s) 1.1 and 1.2. This subroutine, kindly supplied by Augustin Dubrulle of HP Labs, performs a back-looking QR triangularization of a square matrix with one square root per step. It is a well-crafted piece of code that demonstrates many of the difficulties inherent in trying to automatically recognize the design underlying a given piece of source code. We have added statement labels to the executable statements to make it easier to refer to the interesting features.

There are actually five distinct variables, all named "s", in this subroutine. s_1 is computed and used in lines 3–11. s_2 is computed and used in lines 22–27. s_3 is computed and used in lines 28–30. s_4 is computed and used in lines 31–34. s_5 is computed and used in lines 44–52. This code would mean the same thing if all of these variables had different names, or if any of the possible subsets had different names.

Variable name re-use is very common in real applications. While these variables all have the same name, they can be distinguished by their usage.

Some approaches to discovering the design behind a program don't distinguish variables by usage, but by symbol name. These approaches will have trouble analyzing codes like our example.

The loop bounds on lines 2, 14, 32, and 50 are neither constants nor variables, but expressions. All of the loops except the ones on lines 38 and 43 have no step specified, but these two have a step value of -1.

Having loop bounds which are arbitrary arithmetic expressions, or which have non-unity steps, is very common in real applications. While these expressions can be arbitrarily complicated in a program source, they must all resolve to an integer at execution time.

Some approaches to discovering the design behind a program don't deal with loop bounds that aren't constants or simple variables. These approaches will have trouble analyzing codes like our example.

Most of the innermost loops in the subroutine correspond to Level 1 subroutines from the BLAS library (17). The loops on lines 4 and 45 correspond to the DDOT routine. The loops on lines 9 and 50 correspond to the DAXPY routine. The loop on line 32 corresponds to the DSCAL routine.

Modularizing small computations, particularly when there are standard subroutine libraries available to do the work, is very common in real applications. Our example happens to be easy in this respect, since the author chose *not* to use these well-known routines. It could just have easily used library subroutine calls wherever possible, or even worse, used a subset of the BLAS sometimes, and other times coded the equivalent functionality directly.

Some approaches to discovering the design behind a program only work on a single subroutine. These approaches would have trouble analyzing codes like our example, if the standard BLAS routines had been employed.

Within the nested loops found on lines 2–12 and 43–53, there are units of computation that could be independently recognized. These are the statements on lines 3–6 and 44–47 respectively. The claim that these are logical units of computation is confirmed by the fact that they can be replaced by a single subroutine call to a widely used library subroutine.

There are two interesting facets of these computation units. First, they are a set of statements executed under the same control conditions, but are not a part of a single control construct. In each case, there is a prologue statement, and then a loop body. Often real codes have loop epilogues as well. Second, the entire set of statements serves itself as a part of the prologue for another loop nest. The design behind the outer loop nest might also be discovered. If a system were built that not only recognized designs, but actually replaced the code with a more efficient implementation, that system must be capable of assessing the benefit of multiple replacements of overlapping code regions.

Some approaches to discovering the in a program are focussed on loop nests. These approaches will have trouble analyzing codes like our example, since essential elements to determining what the loop is doing actually occur outside the loop nest boundary.

The example we have given in this section should make it easier to understand that the problem of discovering the design behind a program is far more complicated than pattern matching the surface elements of a program. It is also more complicated than many traditional compiler optimizations.

1.4 Technical Issues

The previous discussion has indicated that this book will touch on the semantic analysis and optimization of computer software, through some form of "program understanding." There are a number of general issues that researchers in this field must address, regardless of their technical approaches to this task.

Extent: Will semantic analysis and optimization be performed on expressions, statements, statement groups, loop nests, procedures, or even entire programs?

Ordering: Will different orderings of operands or program statements be recognized as equivalent when they are in fact equivalent?

Variation: Will different choices of programming language constructs be recognized as equivalent when they achieve the same purpose?

Focus: Will there be a mechanism to focus the semantic analysis on program elements that are more important?

```
         subroutine qrb1 ( a, ld, n, h, q, lq )
         integer    ld, n, lq
         real*8     a(ld,n), h(n), q(lq,n)

         integer    i, j, k
         real*8     r, s, t
001  do k=1,n
002     do j=1,k-1
003        s=a(j,k)
004        do i=j+1,n
005           s=s+a(i,j)*a(i,k)
006        end do
007        s=s*h(j)
008        a(j,k)=a(j,k)+s
009        do i=j+1,n
010           a(i,k)=a(i,k)+s*a(i,j)
011        end do
012     end do
013     t=0d0
014     do i=k+1,n
015        t=t+abs(a(i,k))
016     end do
017     if(t.eq.0d0)then
018        h(k)=0d0
019     else
020        t=t+abs(a(k,k))
021        r=1d0/t
022        s=0d0
023        do i=k,n
024           a(i,k)=r*a(i,k)
025           s=s+a(i,k)**2
026        end do
027        r=-sign(sqrt(s),a(k,k))
028        s=a(k,k)-r
029        a(k,k)=t*r
030        h(k)=s/r
031        s=1d0/s
032        do i=k+1,n
033           a(i,k)=s*a(i,k)
034        end do
035     end if
036  end do
037  if (lq.lt.n) return
```

Figure 1.1
QR Triangularization — triangularization phase

Non-Contiguousness: Will the relationship between logically related program elements that were not lexically adjacent be recognized?

```
038   do k=n,1,-1
039      q(k,k)=1d0+h(k)
040      do i=k+1,n
041         q(i,k)=h(k)*a(i,k)
042      end do
043      do j=k-1,1,-1
044         s=0d0
045         do i=j+1,n
046            s=s+a(i,j)*q(i,k)
047         end do
048         s=h(j)*s
049         q(j,k)=s
050         do i=j+1,n
051            q(i,k)=q(i,k)+s*a(i,j)
052         end do
053      end do
054   end do
055   return
056   end
```

Figure 1.2
QR Triangularization — construction of Q phase

Selection: If multiple optimizations are indicated as a result of program analysis, how will the best optimizations be chosen?

Correctness: If the resulting semantic analysis is used to guide optimization, how can the correctness of the transformations be ensured?

Scalability: Will the proposed methods scale to work on real applications (100,000 or more source lines) with a knowledge database large enough (1,000 or more algorithms) to recognize most realizations of the major techniques in use today?

Only the replacement-motivated projects need to be concerned with the correctness. Replacing non-contiguous statements correctly and maintaining the correspondence of identified pattern elements with library parameters are two of the issues they must handle. Similarly, selection is an issue that arises only when a system attempts to perform optimizations.

The remainder of this work is our attempt to create a theoretically sound and computationally viable approach to algorithm recognition and replacement. We seek to address all of the technical issues raised here.

1.5 Prehistory of the Solution

The past often explains the present. In our case, our professional experience prior to the project that resulted in this book provides clues to the motivation and direction that the project took. We have identified the following activities as motivations for our research:

- experiences implementing vectorizing compilers,

- experiences implementing interprocedural compilers,

- interaction with people doing competitive benchmarking,

- interest in compiling APL programs, and

- interest in the results of the Programmer's Apprentice project.

Vectorizing Compilers

In 1988, Convex Computer Corporation began shipping its C-2 series of vector-parallel processors. The Fortran compiler (version 5.0) for that system included a powerful optimizer that performed automatic **vectorization** and **parallelization**.

At that time, the Livermore Loops suite was one of the key benchmarks used to evaluate high performance systems and their compilers. Two of the loops were not vectorizable by standard algorithmic means. The loop computing the partial **prefix sum** of a vector has an actual **recurrence**. The loop searching for the first minimum value of a vector and returning the index has a premature loop exit. Recurrences and loop exits hinder standard vectorization algorithms.

To get the maximum performance on the Livermore loops, the Fortran project leader implemented a special pass after normal vectorization. This pass found two loops that could be partially realized with vector instructions. He described the technique as follows: "The only pattern matching performed by the compiler currently is to recognize recurrences that can in fact be vectorized but not by straightforward methods." (37) Most compilers for high-performance computers contain such techniques for improving their benchmark standing, but vendors are rarely willing to admit it publicly.

The compiler internal representation used **directed graphs** to represent expressions **data flow**, and **control flow**. The pattern matching for the two loops was a cascading series of tests on the arcs and nodes that represented a singly-nested loop. It took 40 tests to identify the vector prefix sum loop and 73 tests to identify the index of minimum search. These counts treat a switch statement as a single test. They also include support for both Fortran and C, since this was a language-independent **optimizer**.

Once the candidate loop was identified, the contents of the loop were removed, the trip count was set to one, and a call to a vectorized runtime library procedure was inserted. Writing the identification and replacement code was time-consuming and error-prone.

Once the Convex pre-sales engineers found out that the compiler could pattern match these two loops, they asked for similar support vectorizing additional similar loops. One of us (Metzger) took over responsibility for the Fortran compiler project after the initial pattern matching work was completed. He added support for matching and replacing two more loop types that had not previously been vectorizable because of premature loop exits:

- searching a vector for the first element of a vector that matches a scalar quantity according to a relation (e.g., equality), and

- searching for the first minimum magnitude value of a vector and returning the index.

It took 80 tests to identify generalized search loops and 71 tests to identify the index of minimum magnitude search. The same caveats apply as with the test counts for the original patterns.

This effort was not purely an exercise in **benchmarking**. Loops that search an array for maximum or minimum values or for an element that meets a certain criterion occur frequently in scientific and engineering applications. Subroutines that implement these loops are found in the standard version of the BLAS (Basic Linear Algebra Subroutine library) (17).

A vendor-supplied version of the BLAS typically runs substantially faster than the version one creates from compiling the public domain sources. If a programmer replaces these loops with calls to the vendor's version of the BLAS, the application will speed up. The procedures called when the loops were pattern matched were special versions of the vendor-supplied BLAS subroutines. So when the compiler matched the loops, the application ran faster without the programmer having to make any changes.

The lack of generality and the labor-intensive nature of the work, however, made it untenable for further development. We wanted an approach to recognizing and replacing patterns that was general and easier to maintain. We believed such an approach required an external **pattern database**. This database would consist of patterns and actions that could be maintained and enhanced without having to change the source code of the compiler itself.

Interprocedural Compilers

In 1991, Convex Computer Corporation began shipping a product, called the Application Compiler, that performed **interprocedural optimization** on programs written in Fortran and C. It was the logical conclusion to a series of increasingly powerful optimizing compilers that became available during the previous two decades. First, compilers performed optimization over a **basic block**, which is a group of sequentially executed statements with a single exit point. Next came compilers that performed optimization over an entire procedure. Finally, compiler technology reached the scope of an entire application.

There were two main motivations for developing this product. The first was to develop new sources of information that would improve **scalar optimization** and vectorization. The second was to automatically parallelize loops that contained procedure calls. With the release of version 2.0 of the Application Compiler at the beginning of 1995, both of these goals were reached.

The Application Compiler performed the following analyses:

- **Call Analysis** – Which procedures are invoked by each call?
- **Alias Analysis** – Which names refer to the same location?
- **Pointer Tracking** – Which pointers point to which locations?
- **Scalar Analysis** – Which procedures (and subordinates) use and assign which scalars?
- **Array Analysis** – Which procedures (and subordinates) use and assign which sections of arrays?

Having a compiler that could automatically parallelize loops that contained procedure calls did expose more high-level parallelism. Unfortunately, it also exposed the inefficiencies in the sequential code that was being parallelized. Some questions naturally arose when this phenomena was observed.

- Could a given sequential algorithm be replaced by another more efficient sequential algorithm?
- Could a given sequential algorithm be replaced by a parallel version of a different algorithm that computes the same result?
- Could a compiler do this automatically?

As the Application Compiler became a mature product, there were few new optimizations that remained to be implemented. Pointer tracking only worked for blocks of contiguous, homogeneous storage. It didn't handle recursive data structures. We considered adding a more general pointer tracking algorithm.

The only other interprocedural optimization it didn't perform was **predicate propagation.** We knew this would be helpful in optimizing both Fortran and C. **Constant propagation** is a special case of predicate propagation, in which the propagated predicate is *variable == constant*. Predicate propagation is a more general optimization. Assertions about the equality of expressions, the monotonicity of sequences, etc. can be related to specific sections of a program.

The department that produced this compiler specialized in compiler optimization. It was clear that we needed to undertake research that would open new doors for optimization. Algorithm recognition seemed to be the most likely candidate.

A programmer can frustrate any algorithm recognition system that works only on a procedural level by hiding some of the details in called procedures. Such modular structure is considered good programming practice. The Application Compiler presented us with a platform for investigating algorithm recognition when dealing with applications written in a modular style.

The results of interprocedural analysis can be used to determine whether a called procedure is relevant to an algorithm to be recognized. If the call is relevant, the procedure can be substituted inline, so that the code executed by the called procedure can be completely analyzed. The Application Compiler had a complete facility for doing this substitution. It also had the infrastructure necessary to use profile information to identify the computational kernels of the application. It became the logical basis for an algorithm recognition project.

Competitive Benchmarking

The peculiar nature of the high-performance computer business also provided a major motivation for investigating automatic algorithm recognition. At some point in the lengthy (six months or more) sales cycle, the customer has narrowed down the prospective vendors to a short list. Some customers only use third-party applications. They will ask the vendors to run these applications on the bid configuration with data sets that represent their workload. If they have written their own applications, they give the vendors the most important of these for porting and execution on the vendors' hardware.

The task of porting and running the application falls to a pre-sales software engineer. The time that this engineer has to get the application running and showing the best performance on the target system is limited. Typically, one to four weeks are allowed. Sometimes as little as a few days are available.

Once the engineer has the application ported and generating correct answers, he or she turns to the problem of optimizing performance. Customers provide a variety of constraints on what can be done at this point. At one extreme, a customer may require that no changes be made to the source code of the application. This makes the benchmark activity as much a test of the compiler's automatic optimization capabilities as the performance of the hardware system. All the engineer can do is specify compiler command-line options, typically stored in a *makefile*.

At the other extreme, the customer may allow the vendors to rewrite any portion of the system they want in assembly language to achieve a performance improvement. This makes the benchmark activity as much a test of the expertise of the benchmarkers as the performance of the hardware system. The sophisticated customers ask for both approaches, in order to evaluate the difference between typical and peak performance.

During application tuning, the engineer often sees unrealized opportunities for performance improvement. The engineer may observe procedures that do the same computation as highly optimized procedures in the vendor's mathematical subroutine library. If the customer's constraint is "no source changes," he or she can't insert a call to the library subroutine. The engineer may observe assembly code generated by the compiler that is slower than what could be written manually. If the customer's constraint is "high-level language source changes only," he or she can't insert a call to an alternative procedure written in hand-polished assembly code.

These circumstances led to regular requests from the Convex pre-sales engineers for compilers that make handling benchmarks simpler. One request was to provide a feature to match user code and replace it with calls to special procedures. These requests led us to see the potential commercial value of an algorithm recognition project.

Such a feature must be usable by a programmer who knows nothing about the internal workings of a compiler. The patterns must be generated directly from high-level language source. The code replacement actions must be a simple specification of a name and a mapping between expressions in the original program and arguments of the special procedure. Adding a new pattern to the knowledge base must be no more complicated than running the compiler with some special command line options.

APL Compilers

One of us (Metzger) had a long-standing interest in the compilation of APL programs. APL is typically interpreted, rather than compiled. This is because, at any point during execution, names can be bound to an object that has a different data type or dimensionality than the previously bound object.

APL interpreters normally operate by preparing operands and executing an operation by dispatching the appropriate runtime subroutine. Several researchers have worked on hybrid interpreter-compilers, or even "pure" compilers for APL (7), since the late 1970's. These compilers typically generate code by composing data structures representing the access patterns of the APL operations into a demand-driven execution model.

These APL compiler efforts have largely focused on optimizing individual statements. This makes sense because APL is a very high level language. A single line of APL can be the equivalent of pages of C or Fortran.

There are several kinds of interpretive overhead within a statement that such compilers can reduce:

- checking operand types before each operation,

- converting operands to the correct type,
- dispatching the correct runtime procedure for a given operation,
- allocating temporary storage for results, and
- copying values to and from temporary variables holding results.

What is not optimized are the actual operations themselves.

APL interpreters are typically coded so that individual operations on an array are just as efficient as any compiled code. An APL interpreter makes a series of calls to runtime subroutines, even for a single statement. An APL compiler replaces those calls with a single call to a procedure generated to execute the equivalent of that line of APL code.

One of the well-known characteristics of APL is the use of **idioms** (39). "An idiom is a construction used by programmers for a logically primitive operation for which no language primitive exists." (47)

Most APL interpreters provide very limited support for idiom recognition. The APL grammar is simple enough that it is often analyzed with a finite state machine. Those idioms that can be recognized during the syntax analysis are replaced with calls to runtime procedures that are not directly accessible to the user.

Snyder's paper on "Recognition and Selection of Idioms for Code Optimization" suggested an alternative approach to compiling APL (47). He describes an algorithm to find idioms in an expression by tree matching. If his approach is used to implement a line of APL with a call to a single runtime procedure, it provides the same order of execution speedup as the other compilation model.

The advantage of Snyder's approach is that it is extensible by the user. If a line of APL code is a performance bottleneck, the user can add a pattern for the idiom in the pattern database, and a procedure that implements it in the runtime library. Snyder's paper inspired us to reconsider trees as a representation for algorithm recognition, when the consensus approach favored graphs.

Programmer's Apprentice

The MIT Programmer's Apprentice project studied how software engineers build software systems and how the various development tasks could be automated. One of the fundamental concepts developed by this project is that of **inspection methods**. "Inspection methods are based on knowledge of commonly used combinations of components, called **cliches**. These cliches form the bulk of the knowledge shared by expert engineers in any domain." (46)

Within the domain of software engineering, they developed the concept of **program plans**. Plans are a canonically-formed, language-independent representation of a computation. All control flow and data flow are explicitly represented as arcs in a graph. In the

Programmer's Apprentice, cliches are represented by plans. Representing the data and control flow of a program with directed graphs is very similar to the internal representation of the Application Compiler.

One of the sub-projects in the Programmer's Apprentice effort was a tool called GRASPR, which was designed to perform program recognition (52). Wills views **program recognition** as a process in which a programmer recognizes parts of a program's design through two activities. He or she identifies cliches and builds a hierarchical description of the design from the use of abstractions that use the cliches.

In Wills' dissertation, she demonstrated that her system could recognize plans in two simulation programs. Wills' GRASPR work showed us that a proof-of-concept system to perform design reconstruction (program recognition) could be built. Her proof-of-concept encouraged us to consider attacking the related problem of optimization by algorithm recognition and replacement. Her proof that her approach of graph parsing is NP complete influenced us to consider alternative methods.

Conclusions

Our prior experience in developing compilers for Convex and our personal research interests led us to the following conclusions.

• Vectorizing by ad hoc pattern matching showed us that pattern matching was useful for optimization. It must, however, be driven by a database of patterns and actions external to the compiler in order to be maintainable.

• Developing an interprocedural optimizing compiler showed us that automatic algorithmic parallelization would expose inferior sequential algorithms. It also showed us that it was possible to deal with obstacles to algorithm recognition through program transformations.

• Experience with competitive benchmarking showed us that algorithm recognition could be commercially valuable.

• APL compiler research, Snyder's work (47) in particular, inspired us to reconsider trees as a representation for algorithm recognition, when the consensus approach favored graphs.

• Wills' part of the Programmer's Apprentice project inspired us to consider attacking the more difficult problem of optimization by algorithm recognition and replacement.

1.6 Outline

The rest of the chapters are organized as follows.

In Chap. 2, we formally define the problem to be solved, and present theoretical results on its inherent difficulties. We also propose a practical solution to the problem.

In Chap. 3, we survey related work in the field of "program understanding", both display-oriented projects as well as replacement-motivated projects.

In Chap. 4, we explain the sources of program variation. We also propose an approach to using compiler transformations that reduce or eliminate these variations.

In Chap. 5, we present the internal representation our approach uses for computational kernels and for algorithm patterns.

In Chap. 6, we present algorithms and heuristics for converting the trees we use to represent programs into a canonical order.

In Chap. 7, we explain how to match the trees we use to represent computational kernels and algorithm patterns.

In Chap. 8, we discuss how to extract statements from a computational kernel to be matched against algorithm patterns.

In Chap. 9, we discuss how to identify a feasible set of algorithm replacements in a computational kernel.

In Chap. 10, we explain how to select replacements that can be applied to maximize performance improvements.

In Chap. 11, we discuss how to perform a set of algorithm replacements in a computational kernel.

In Chap. 12, we present a comprehensive analysis of the time complexity of our algorithms.

In Chap. 13, we present some conclusions, other applications of our ideas, and areas for further research.

In Appendix A, we present the high-level architecture of a software system that could implement the ideas in this book. Appendix B gives the detailed module design of the algorithm recognition and replacement part of the system. Appendix C describes the input required by such a system. In Appendix D, we present some statistics regarding the characteristics of our heuristics.

2 The Problem and Its Complexity

In this chapter, we formally define the problem to be solved, and present theoretical results on its inherent difficulties. We then propose a practical solution to the problem.

2.1 The Problem and the Ideal Solution

Our goal is to identify computationally intensive (or more generally, resource intensive) groups of statements in a program and to replace them with semantically equivalent library procedure calls that are more efficient.

This goal immediately raises one question that can only be resolved by actually executing the program. Which procedures, including the procedures they call directly or indirectly, use the majority of the computational or other resource we seek to optimize?

The question can be answered by using the following process. What results is the identification of the **computational kernel** of the program.

1. Compile the application for profiling.

2. Execute the application under the control of a profiler. The profiler must be able to generate a dynamic call graph. Examples include the *gprof* utility (20) found on many UNIX(tm) systems or the *CXperf* tool (11) available on Hewlett-Packard computer systems.

3. Use test data sets that reflect typical usage.

4. Review the profile results and identify those procedures that used a significant fraction of the execution time. These are the **kernel roots**.

5. Review the dynamic call graph and identify all procedures that were invoked, either directly or indirectly, by the kernel roots.

6. All procedures identified in this process together comprise the computational kernel of the application.

An ideal solution to achieve our goal must resolve the following issues and questions precisely. The first question concerns recognition. The rest concern replacement.

1. Which groups of statements (not necessarily contiguous) are semantically equivalent to which library procedure calls with what actual parameters?

2. Replacing a group of statements that are originally non-contiguous by a library procedure call could violate the semantics of the program. This can happen even if these statements together by themselves are semantically equivalent to the library call. What is the condition under which such a replacement is valid?

3. It is possible that many groups of statements are semantically equivalent to several different library procedure calls. If these groups overlap, simultaneously replacing each of these groups by a library procedure call may not always be valid, or even possible. Even if these replacements do not overlap, and each replacement is valid when applied alone, it may still be invalid to apply them altogether. What is the condition under which multiple replacements are valid?

4. Different replacements may result in different improvements in performance (e.g., run time). For optimization purpose, what is the best set of replacements to maximize performance improvements?

5. How can the replacements be carried out?

Before we attempt any solution to the remaining questions, let us be precise about semantic equivalence.

DEFINITION 2.1:   **Subprogram:** A subprogram is a list of statements, probably extracted from a larger program. Variables occurring in the statements are called **computational variables**. All variables are considered parameters of the subprogram. This includes both computational variables as well as those only used in specifying the data types of other variables. **Output parameters**, if any, are those variables that are defined (receive values) in the subprogram. **Input parameters**, if any, are the variables whose values are defined outside the subprogram are used in the subprogram.   ■

It is very important to point out that we may consider subprograms and programs in a language-independent **intermediate representation**, rather than source code.

Each variable in the subprogram has a data type, such as integer or logical. In Def. 2.1, a variable can be a scalar, an array, or even an external file used in read/write statements. A parameter can be both an input parameter and an output parameter of the subprogram, in which case we call it an **input&output parameter**. It is possible that some parameters do not appear in executable statements. For example, as in many Fortran procedures, sometimes a parameter is only used to specify the size of another array parameter.

A **procedure** definition associates an identifier with one or more statements. In Fortran, subroutines and functions are procedures. In C, functions are procedures. All procedures are subprograms, but not all subprograms are procedures.

DEFINITION 2.2:   **Semantic Equivalence:** Let P and P' be two subprograms with the same number of parameters. We define P and P' to be semantically equivalent if and only if there is a listing or ordering of the parameters of P and P' as $P(I_1, ..., I_r, IO_1, ..., IO_s, O_1, ..., O_t)$, and $P'(I'_1, ..., I'_r, IO'_1, ..., IO'_s, O'_1, ..., O'_t)$, where I_i and I'_i ($i = 1, ...r$) are input parameters of the same type, if any. IO_j and IO'_j ($j = 1, ...s$) are input&output parameters of the same type, if any. O_k and O'_k ($k = 1, ..., t$) are output parameters of the same type, if any, such that the following condition is true:

Whenever P and P' are invoked with $I_i = I'_i$ and $IO_j = IO'_j$ (for all $1 \leq i \leq r$ and $1 \leq j \leq s$), then either

(1) both P and P' will not halt, or

(2) both P and P' will halt, and when they halt we will have $O_k = O'_k$ and $IO_j = IO'_j$ (for all $1 \leq k \leq t$ and $1 \leq j \leq s$).

In other words, given the same input, their output will always be the same. ∎

Semantic equivalence is an equivalence relation between subprograms. It is easy to verify that it is reflexive, symmetric, and transitive.

Determining the semantic equivalence of any pair of subprograms is an unsolvable problem, for two reasons.

1. There is no algorithm that determines, for every subprogram and input, whether the subprogram halts on the given input. This is the well-known Turing machine halting problem.

2. Even if we know that both subprograms P and P' halt for input from a domain, it is still undecidable whether their output will always be the same. It is an unsolvable problem just to determine whether their output will ever be the same.

The second part is stated in the following lemma and corollary.

LEMMA 2.1:   There is no algorithm that determines, for every domain D and every sub-program $F(I_1, ..., I_r, O_1)$ halting on all input $(I_1, ..., I_r) \in D$, whether $F(I_1, ..., I_r, O_1)$ will ever return the constant zero, i.e. $O_1 = 0$.

Proof. Should such an algorithm exist, we would be able to use it to determine whether a subprogram of the following form will ever return zero.

```
SUBPROGRAM F(I₁, ..., Iᵣ, O₁)
    if (E(I₁, ..., Iᵣ) = 0) then
        O₁ = 0;
    else
        O₁ = 1;
END
```

In other words, such an algorithm could determine, for any expression $E(I_1, ..., I_r)$, whether equation $E(I_1, ..., I_r) = 0$ has any solutions. However, it is known that "there is no algorithm that determines, for any exponential **diophantine equation**, whether the equation has any solutions" (19). ■

COROLLARY 2.1: There is no algorithm that determines, for every domain D and every pair of subprograms $F(I_1, ..., I_r, O_1)$ and $F'(I_1, ..., I_r, O_1)$ known to halt on all input from $(I_1, ..., I_r) \in D$, whether $F(I_1, ..., I_r, O_1)$ and $F'(I_1, ..., I_r, O_1)$ will ever produce identical output.

Proof. Let $F'(I_1, ..., I_r, O_1)$ be a subprogram that always returns constant zero. By the previous lemma, the conclusion follows. ■

Now we know that it is impossible to develop a general algorithm or tool that can determine whether a subprogram is semantically equivalent to any of the procedures in a library. In other words, the recognition part of our goal cannot be achieved 100%. This doesn't prevent us, however, from solving it at least partially.

2.2 Algorithm Recognition and Replacement

Instead of trying to determine the semantic equivalence of subprograms in general, we shall concentrate on subprograms implementing the same algorithm. Our fundamental approach is algorithm pattern matching, which by our definition is algorithmic instance testing. Here, an algorithmic instance, to be defined later, is a binary relation between subprograms. Algorithmic instance testing determines whether such a relation exists between two subprograms.

The problem now becomes algorithm recognition and replacement. The first part, algorithm recognition, is defined in terms algorithmic instance testing. In particular, it involves determining which groups of statements, not necessarily contiguous, in a computational kernel are algorithmic instances of which algorithm patterns in a database. The second part, algorithm replacement, resolves all the replacement related issues, as listed at the beginning of Sect. 2.1.

Our approach "extracts" statements from a given computational kernel. These statements, treated together as a subprogram, called the **extracted subprogram**, are then compared with the algorithm patterns, e.g. subprograms.

Algorithm pattern matching determines whether this extracted subprogram is an algorithmic instance of any member in a database of algorithm patterns. If the subprogram is found to be an algorithmic instance of one of the pattern subprograms, we know what problem this subprogram is to solve. The subprogram may then be replaced by a call to a library procedure designed to solve the same problem, but more efficiently. Our approach can determine which replacements are validly performed together, select the best set of replacements to maximize performance improvements, and carry out the replacements automatically.

In our approach, before a computational kernel is processed by the algorithm recognition and replacement system, it will first be put through a preprocessing phase. This performs a series of **semantics-preserving transformations** using an optimizing compiler to reduce program variations. The advantage of having the preprocessing is to cut down the number of algorithm patterns to be maintained in the databases because of program variation. The causes of program variation and the semantics-preserving transformations to reduce them are listed in Chap. 4.

Our definition of algorithm pattern matching is to check whether a subprogram is an algorithmic instance of another subprogram. In the rest of this section, we shall define precisely algorithm pattern matching. We also shall discuss its inherent theoretical difficulties and our approach to solve it.

Algorithmic Equivalence

DEFINITION 2.3:   **Algorithmic Equivalence:** Let P and P' be two subprograms. Define P and P' to be algorithmically equivalent if and only if one can be obtained from the other through following transformations.

- **Rename** the variables. The renaming is done in such a way that all occurrences of the same name will be renamed to the same new name, and that different names will still be different after renaming. We shall call this **one-to-one renaming**.
- **Reorder** the statements without violating the semantics.
- **Permute** the operands of any **commutative operator**. ∎

Algorithmic equivalence is an equivalence relation between subprograms. It is easy to verify that it is reflexive, symmetric, and transitive. For example, the two loops in Fig. 2.1, considered as subprograms, are algorithmically equivalent.

We need two more notations before we can define the concept of algorithmic instance.

Induction Values

DEFINITION 2.4:   **Induction Value:** Let LP be a loop. An induction value (**i-val** for short) IV in loop LP is an integer quantity that is incremented by the same loop constant,

```
integer i,n,k
real A(n),B(n),C(n),D(n)
real E(n),F(n),G(n)

do i = 1, k
  A(i) = B(i)*C(i)+D(i)
  E(i) = F(i)+G(i)
enddo
```

```
integer j, m,k
real X(m),Y(m),Z(m)
real T(m),U(m),V(m),W(m)

do j = 1, k
  X(j) = Y(j)+Z(j)
  T(j) = U(j)+V(j)*W(j)
enddo
```

Figure 2.1
Algorithmically equivalent loops

relative to LP, on every iteration of LP. We say that i-val IV belongs to loop LP. An i-val can only belong to one loop. ∎

An i-val has a three parts:

- a uniquely determined starting value,
- an increment, often called the step, which is a loop constant, and
- a final value that can be derived from the previous two and the number of iterations of the enclosing loop nest.

An i-val can best be represented by a triplet ($begin$, end, $step$). If the number of iterations is not computable when the loop starts, the second component of triplet is NULL.

Our definition of induction value is slightly more general than the conventional definition of induction variable (2). A conventional induction variable always corresponds directly to a variable in the source code, while our induction value does not necessarily do so. A conventional induction variable is also an induction value by our definition, but not vice versa.

Induction values are often related to **loop control variables** and array subscript expressions. For implementation purposes, i-vals are given **identifications** by the compiler. An i-val is referenced through a pointer to its identification. In our notation, we shall use (?I) to identify an i-val. Consider the example in Fig. 2.2.

This example has the following i-vals.

```
k = 0
do i = 1, n, 1
  A(k) = ...
  do j = 1, m, 1
    B(j) = ...
    C(i*j) = ...
    D(i+2*j) = ...
    E(k) = ...
    k = k+5
  enddo
enddo
```

Figure 2.2
I-vals originate in several ways

?I1: $(1, n, 1)$: This i-val is related to loop control variable i, and it belongs to loop do-i.

?I2: $(1, m, 1)$: This i-val is related to loop control variable j, and also to the subscript of $B(j)$, and it belongs to loop do-j.

?I3: $(0, 5 * m * n, 5 * m)$: This i-val is related to the subscript of $A(k)$, and it belongs to loop do-i.

?I4: $((?I1), (?I1) * m, (?I1))$: This i-val is related to the subscript of $C(i * j)$, and it belongs to loop do-j.

?I5: $((?I1) + 2, (?I1) + 2 * m, 2)$: This i-val is related to the subscript of $D(i + 2 * j)$, and it belongs to loop do-j.

?I6: $((?I3), (?I3) + 5 * m, 5)$: This i-val is related to the subscript of $E(k)$, and it belongs to loop do-j.

Type Expressions

For the purpose of **type checking**, a concept called the **type expression** is introduced in (2, pp. 345–380) to describe the data type of a language construct. A type expression is either a basic type or is formed by applying an operator called a **type constructor** to other type expressions. The sets of basic types and constructors are language dependent. The type constructors include **array of**, **pointer to**, etc.

Typically, the basic types are **integer**, **logical**, **character**, and **real**. There are multiple versions of these types to accommodate single and double word realizations of the numeric types, and varying length strings of the character types.

For our purpose of algorithm pattern matching of Fortran and C programs, we define this concept as follows.

DEFINITION 2.5:   **Type Expression:** A type expression is an expression, in which

vector is the only **non-commutative** operator, and the operands are literal constants **integer** or **logical**, etc.), integer constants, integer variables, and a special symbol **?** called the **wildcard**. ■

The data type of each variable in the program can be described using a type expression. Two variables are considered to have the same data type if and only if they have the same type expression. An example of type expressions for Fortran is shown in Fig. 2.3. Figure 2.4 gives an example of type expressions for C.

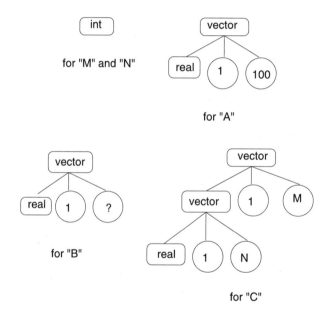

Figure 2.3
Type expressions for Fortran variables INTEGER M,N and REAL A(100), B(*),C(M,N)

DEFINITION 2.6:   **Type Instantiation:** A type expression TE' is an instantiation of type expression TE if TE' can be obtained from TE through the following transformations.

- **Rename** the variables. The renaming is done in such a way that all occurrences of the same name will be renamed to the same new name, and that different names will still be different after renaming.
- **Substitute** all occurrences of a variable with an integer constant.

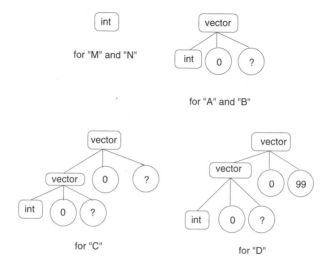

Figure 2.4
Type expressions for C variables int M,N, A[], *B, **C, *D[100]

- **Substitute** any wildcard symbol ? with an integer constant or with an integer variable.

The way the variables of TE are renamed or substituted to obtain TE' is referred to as **constraints** for TE' to be an instantiation of TE. ∎

Let v_1, ..., v_s be the variables in TE, and u_1, ..., u_t be the variables in TE'. The constraints can best be expressed as $v_i = \alpha_i$ (for $i = 1, ..., s$), where α_i is either an integer constant or u_j (for some $1 \leq j \leq t$).

We have already defined the notion of algorithmic equivalence. Allowing a little bit more than reordering and renaming, we can define another concept, algorithmic instance.

Algorithmic Instance

DEFINITION 2.7:   **Algorithmic Instance:** Let P and P' be two subprograms. P' is called an algorithmic instance of P if and only if P' can be obtained from P through the following transformations.

- **Rename** the computational variables through one-to-one renaming. Renaming a computational variable X to X' is allowed only when the data type of X' can be made into an instantiation of the data type of X.
- **Reorder** the statements without violating the semantics.
- **Permute** the operands of any commutative operator.

• **Substitute** all occurrences of a computational variable X with a function $f(y_1, ..., y_s)$. This substitution is allowed only when X is NOT used anywhere BUT in the initializations, the increments, or the final-limits of some induction values. Furthermore, all variable substitutions must be done simultaneously.

• Finally, after substitution of computational variables with functions, perform arithmetic simplifications only on those initializations, increments, and final-limits that are affected by the substitutions.

Let $x_1, ..., x_m$ be the variables in P, and $y_1, ..., y_n$ be the variables in P'. The way the variables of P are renamed or substituted to obtain P' is best expressed as $x_i = f_i(y_1, y_2, ..., y_n)$ (for $i = 1, ..., m$). We will refer to these as **constraints** for P' to match, or be an algorithmic instance of, P. These constraints include those for the data type instantiations. ■

Algorithmic instance is a binary relation between subprograms. This binary relation is reflexive and transitive, but it is not symmetric.

In the example in Fig. 2.5, the lower subprogram is an algorithmic instance of the upper subprogram under the constraints $L = 1$, $H = M/N + 1$, $S = 5$, $A = T$, $B = V$, $C = W$, and $D = U$. Information about the data types of the variables may be implicit if the subprogram is extracted from a larger program.

```
integer I,L,H,S
real A(*),B(*),C(*),D(*)

do I= L, H, S
  A(I)= B(I) * C(I) + D(I)
enddo
```

```
integer J,M,N
real T(*),U(*),V(*),W(*)

do J= 1, M/N+1, 5
  T(J)= U(J) + V(J) * W(J)
enddo
```

Figure 2.5
Algorithmic instance

A careful reader may notice that, by Def. 2.3 and 2.7, the two subprograms in Fig. 2.6 are not algorithmically equivalent, nor is one an algorithmic instance of the other. Program analysis must respect parentheses put in by the programmers, as the Fortran standard requires Fortran compilers to do. $b * c + b * d$ and $b * (c + d)$ can have different numerical precision, depending on the hardware architecture, floating point system used, etc.

```
integer I,N
real A(*),B(*),C(*),D(*)

do I= 1, N
  A(I)= B(I)*C(I)+B(I)*D(I)
enddo
```

```
integer I,N
real A(*),B(*),C(*),D(*)

do I= 1, N
  A(I)= B(I)*(C(I)+D(I))
enddo
```

Figure 2.6
Parentheses operator and algorithmic instances

In the example in Fig. 2.7, the lower subprogram is not an algorithmic instance of the upper subprogram, nor are they algorithmically equivalent. This is because one can never be obtained from the other by one-to-one renaming of the computational variables. For implementation purpose, a special case like of the lower subprogram will have to be maintained as a separate pattern if we want to have both.

```
integer I,N
real A(*),B(*),C(*)

do I= 1, N
  A(I)= B(I) * C(I)
enddo
```

```
integer I,N
real A(*),B(*)

do I= 1, N
  A(I)= B(I) * B(I)
enddo
```

Figure 2.7
Multiple variable roles and algorithmic instances

In the example in Fig. 2.8, the lower subprogram is not an algorithmic instance of the upper subprogram, nor are they algorithmically equivalent. This is because one can never be obtained from the other by one-to-one renaming of the computational variables. In particular, Y cannot be renamed to both B and C at the same time. This example demonstrates the importance of the consistency of the constraints during algorithmic instance testing.

```
real X(*),Y(*)
integer I

do I= 1, 100
  X(I) = Y(I)+Y(I)*Y(I)
enddo
```

```
real A(*),B(*),C(*)
integer I

do I= 1, 100
  A(I) = B(I)+C(I)*C(I)
enddo
```

Figure 2.8
Constraint consistency in algorithmic instance testing

In the example in Fig. 2.9, the lower subprogram is not an algorithmic instance of the upper subprogram, nor are they algorithmically equivalent. This is because one can never be obtained from the other by one-to-one renaming. The inconsistent types of the computational variables could result in numerical differences. This example demonstrates the importance of the the the consistency of the constraints during algorithmic instance testing.

We can replace a given subprogram $I(y_1, y_2, ..., y_t)$ with a library procedure call, if we know two things. First, subprogram I is an algorithmic instance of one of the pattern subprograms P in a pattern database. Second, subprogram I matches pattern P under a completely determined set of constraints.

Consider programs and library procedures written in Fortran. Assume that subprogram $I(y_1, y_2, ..., y_t)$ is an algorithmic instance of pattern subprogram $P(x_1, ..., x_s)$, for which the parameters are renamed and substituted as $x_i = f_i(y_1, y_2, ..., y_t)$ $(i = 1, 2, ..., s)$. We know that subprogram $P(f_1(y_1, y_2, ..., y_t), ..., f_s(y_1, y_2, ..., y_t))$ and $I(y_1, y_2, ..., y_t)$ are semantically equivalent. Recall that our goal is to replace I with a call to a library procedure that is more efficient. Since we know what pattern subprogram $P(x_1, ..., x_s)$ is supposed to do, we write a library procedure that does the same thing using the most effi-

```
real*8 X(*),Y(*)
real*4 Z(*)
integer I

do I= 1, 100
  Z(I)= sqrt(X(I)*Y(I))
enddo
```

```
real*8 A(*),B(*),C(*)
integer I

do I= 1, 100
  C(I)= sqrt(B(I)*C(I))
enddo
```

Figure 2.9
Type consistency in algorithmic instance testing

cient algorithm available. Let $PP(x_1, ..., x_s)$ be such a library procedure. We can replace $I(y_1, y_2, ..., y_t)$ with library procedure call $PP(f_1(y_1, ..., y_t), ..., f_s(y_1, y_2, ..., y_t))$. This suggests the approach that we can use to get to our goal.

Inherent Difficulties of Algorithmic Instance Testing and Algorithm Recognition

We will now discuss how to solve the problem of determining whether a subprogram is an algorithmic instance of another, and how to solve the algorithm recognition problem. First we will consider the inherent complexities of these problems.

If we have a tool to determine for any pair of subprograms, whether one is an algorithmic instance of the other under what constraints, such a tool can also be used to determine whether the two subprograms are algorithmically equivalent. Therefore, it is harder to develop such a tool, or a general algorithm, for algorithmic instance testing than algorithmic equivalence testing. How hard is the problem of algorithmic equivalence testing? Before we answer this, let us consider the graph isomorphism problem and the subgraph isomorphism problem.

DEFINITION 2.8:   **Graph Isomorphism Testing:** ((45)) For any two graphs, determine whether there is a **bijective mapping** from the nodes of one graph to the nodes of the other graph such that the edge connections are respected.   ■

The graph isomorphism problem is a long-standing open problem. Until now, the graph isomorphism problem is still unsolved in the sense that no polynomially-bounded algorithm for it has yet been found. It has been conjectured that no such algorithm can exist (45). On the other hand, no NP-completeness proof for graph isomorphism, nor any other arguments for its intractability have been obtained either. (For good surveys, refer to (45) and (30).)

DEFINITION 2.9:   **Subgraph Isomorphism Testing:** ((21)) Given two graphs G and H, determine whether G contains a subgraph isomorphic to H.   ■

The subgraph isomorphism testing problem is known to be NP-complete (21).

THEOREM 2.1:   Algorithmic equivalence testing of any two subprograms is at least as difficult as graph isomorphism testing.

Proof. The graph isomorphism problem is known to be equivalent to many other restricted isomorphism problems, such as **rooted directed acyclic graph** isomorphism (1) (45). To prove that algorithmic equivalence testing is at least as difficult as the graph isomorphism problem, we only need to show how the rooted directed acyclic graph isomorphism problem can be reduced to algorithmic equivalence testing.

Let G be a rooted directed acyclic graph. Let $v_1, v_2, ..., v_n$ be a topological order of the vertices of G, where v_1 must be the root of G. The induced subprogram P of graph G is defined as follows. P consists of a sequence of n assignment statements $x_1 = y$, $x_2 = E_2$, $x_3 = E_3, ..., x_n = E_n$, where each E_i ($2 \leq i \leq n$) is a simple expression containing only the operator "+" and some of the variables $x_1, x_2, ..., x_n$. Variable v_j ($1 \leq j \leq i - 1$) appears in E_i if and only if (v_j, v_i) is an arc in G. G can be seen as the P's **data flow dependence graph**. (Refer to (58) for the definition of data flow dependence graph.)

Let G_1 and G_2 be two rooted directed acyclic graphs. Let P_1 and P_2 be their induced subprograms. It is easy to see that G_1 and G_2 are isomorphic if and only if P_1 and P_2 are algorithmically equivalent.   ■

Algorithmic instance testing is very difficult, if solvable at all, in general. The functions substituting the variables, used in the i-vals, can be arbitrary. Even when these substituting functions are simple (e.g., linear functions), algorithmic equivalence testing is still a special case of algorithmic instance testing. So the following corollary is obvious.

COROLLARY 2.2:   Algorithmic instance testing is at least as difficult as graph isomorphism testing.   ■

We have already defined, at the beginning of Sect. 2.2, that algorithm recognition is to determine which groups of statements in a program are algorithmic instances of which algorithm pattern subprograms in a database. Similar to the proof of Thm. 2.1, it is easy to reduce the problem of subgraph isomorphism testing to the problem of algorithm recognition. Using a similar reduction technique, the **Program Understanding Problem** was shown in (55) to be NP-hard. Therefore, we have the following theorem.

THEOREM 2.2:   The algorithm recognition problem is at least as difficult as the problem of subgraph isomorphism testing, which is NP-hard.   ■

The Basic Approach to Algorithmic Instance Testing and Algorithm Recognition

Our definition of algorithm pattern matching is to do algorithmic instance testing. Given the inherent difficulty of algorithmic instance testing, we shall not try to develop an algorithm that works for all possible cases. Since we seek an approach that can be the basis of a system that programmers can use in software development, we cannot afford to use an algorithm that solves the problem by exhaustive enumerations (such as graph parsing (52)). The alternative will be to develop heuristic algorithms that are strong enough to cover most of the cases in practice.

We want to be certain about one thing. When we find an extracted subprogram to be an algorithmic instance of one of the patterns, it will be a real match. Therefore, when we later decide to replace the extracted subprogram with a library call, such a replacement will be semantically correct.

To check whether one subprogram is an algorithmic instance of the other, we need to do the following.

1. Compare the control flow structures of the subprograms.

2. Compare the conditions dominating the corresponding branches in the control flow, due to conditional statements and while-loops. Whenever necessary, compare the type expressions of the corresponding variables.

3. Compare the corresponding simple statements. Whenever necessary, compare the type expressions of the corresponding variables.

4. Compare the corresponding i-vals. By doing this, the corresponding loop counters for Fortran DO-loops are compared, so are some of the corresponding array subscripts. For array subscripts that are not i-vals, they will be compared as expressions.

It is worth pointing out that there is no need to compare the data flow dependence structures explicitly. This will be done implicitly through comparisons and renaming of variables.

Similarly to the problem of algorithm recognition, we cannot afford to extract all possible combinations of statements and do algorithmic instance testing for each combination.

There are too many such combinations. Instead, we shall develop heuristics for extraction based on the types of statements, the control flow as well as the topological properties of data flow dependence graphs for the statements. Once again, the heuristic algorithms need to be efficient and strong enough to handle most of the cases in practice.

2.3 Summary

- We seek to identify computationally intensive sections of a program and replace them with semantically equivalent library procedure calls.
- Determining the semantic equivalence of any pair of subprograms is an unsolvable problem.
- Our solution is to perform algorithm pattern matching.
- Algorithm instance testing is an expanded form of algorithm equivalence testing.
- Algorithm pattern matching determines whether a subprogram is an algorithm instance of any member of a database of algorithm patterns.
- Algorithm instance testing is at least as difficult as graph isomorphism testing.

3 Related Work

3.1 Overview

This chapter surveys and evaluates a variety of projects related to our work that can be roughly categorized as Program Understanding efforts.

We divide these projects into two groups. The first group, display-motivated projects, seek to help a programmer understand a program. They attempt to do this by recognizing abstractions in the code and displaying this information in a textual or graphical output.

The second group, replacement-motivated projects, seek to improve the execution performance of a program. They attempt to do this by automatically recognizing abstractions in the code and replacing the identified code with other code that has better performance characteristics.

In one sense, our project falls into the second group. We seek to improve application performance as these other projects do. On the other hand, we have a radically different formulation of the problem. None of these other projects have a formal and exact definition of what they seek to replace. Consequently, they describe the problem in terms of their particular solution. In the previous chapter, we presented a formal and exact definition of the problem we seek to solve.

We describe the projects as presented in their various publications. We evaluate these efforts based on the criteria of the technical issues we raised in Sect. 1.4.

3.2 Display-Motivated Projects

Wills' GRASPR

The purpose of Wills' work (52) (53) is to investigate the feasibility of **graph parsing** for automating program recognition. She defines program recognition as the process of recognizing cliched computational structures, relating them to more abstract structures, and building a hierarchical description of a program's design. She envisions this technique as one of many required for a program understanding system. Such a system will be an interactive system, in which the human engineer provides guidance and information.

Wills describes the system architecture as follows (53).

"GRASPR employs a graph parsing approach to automating program recognition ... It represents a program as a restricted form of directed acyclic graph, called a flow graph ..., which is annotated with attributes. Nodes in the flow graph represent functions, edges denote data flow, and attributes capture control flow information. The cliche library is encoded as an attributed graph grammar, whose rules impose constraints on the attributes of flow graphs matching the rules' right-hand sides. Recognition is achieved by parsing the data flow graph in accordance with the grammar."

The parser maintains a chart of partial and complete analyses of the input graphs in the form of items. The parser repeatedly creates new items by extending partial items with complete items for unmatched nodes. **Constraints** not only ensure correctness, but provide some pruning of the search space. There are constraints on node types (functions), edge connections (data flow), and co-occurrence of functions that must be executed under the same control flow conditions.

We evaluate Wills' work based on the technical issues discussed in Chap. 1 as follows.

- **Extent:** GRASPR deals with whole programs by substituting called procedures inline.

- **Ordering:** GRASPR used graph parsing to exhaustively consider all orders of connected nodes. Exhaustive enumeration is effective but not efficient, because the number of possibilities is exponential.

- **Variation:** GRASPR reduces some types of variation by converting programs to a flow graph representation.

- **Focus:** GRASPR is part of an interactive system, and plans were made to allow a user to identify items to search for.

- **Non-contiguousness:** GRASPR relies on a graph representation for programs to connect elements that are related by data or control flow, but are not lexically contiguous.

- **Scalability:** Wills proved that flow graph parsing is NP complete. The clear implication is that the method does not scale well.

- **Selection:** Like all display-oriented projects, GRASPR does not have to handle the selection problem.

- **Correctness:** Like all display-oriented projects, GRASPR does not have to handle the correctness problem.

Harandi and Ning's PAT

The purpose of Harandi and Ning's work (22) is to support software maintainers. They intend to provide information on the high-level concepts a piece of code contains, the mapping of low-level concepts to the actual implementation, and incorrectly implemented low-level concepts. The technical approach of the system is a deductive inference-rule engine.

Both syntactic and semantic information are subsumed in what the authors term a **program event**. Events have control and lexical intervals. The former determines where the event is in the control path when the code is executed. The latter determines where the event is in the nested hierarchy of the program text. The control and lexical requirements of an event, together with an event's special constraints, determine whether a rule fires. When these are satisfied, a new event is created.

Synthesis of higher-level concepts results when new events are inferred from existing ones using plan rules stored in a plan database. Plan rules are triggered by events defined in a plan's event requirements. The system can generate natural-language descriptions from concepts it has identified or synthesized. There are no apparent application domain specific features.

We evaluate Harandi and Ning's work based on the technical issues discussed in Chap. 1 as follows.

- **Extent:** It appears that the tool at least processes multiple procedures in a single source file, if not multiple source files, but this is never explicitly stated.
- **Ordering:** The authors do not mention this problem or a solution.
- **Variation:** The authors do not mention this problem or a solution. They say that a language parser and simple control-flow analyzer provide the input to the "event base". These features do not provide the transformational power necessary to deal with most sources of variation.
- **Focus:** This is an interactive system. The authors don't mention any automatic focus mechanism.
- **Non-contiguousness:** The authors mention using event-path expressions "to categorize classes of equivalent event sequences, which may not be lexically adjacent." They do not explain how this feature deals with the non-contiguousness problem.
- **Selection:** Like all display-oriented projects, PAT does not have to handle the selection problem.
- **Correctness:** Like all display-oriented projects, PAT does not have to handle the correctness problem.
- **Scalability:** The scalability of the system will be limited by the performance of the pattern-directed inference engine. The authors do not present a complexity analysis, nor enough data to make inferences about its complexity.

An important limitation of most display approaches is stated by the authors.

"The reasoning procedure in PAT is less formal than that used in other deduction, transformation, parsing, or graph-matching approaches. A PAT analysis cannot rigorously prove anything because it is a selective inspection, not a total reduction of a program."

On the other hand, replacement-motivated approaches cannot perform a replacement of a code segment that has been partially recognized.

Biggerstaff's DESIRE

The purpose of Biggerstaff's work (5) (6) is to recognize concepts within a program. This enables the system to build an understanding of the program by relating the recognized concepts to portions of the program and the context in which it operates. The automatic recognition component (DM-TAO) is embedded in an interactive system that provides "naive assistant" facilities such as program slicing.

The DM-TAO intelligent assistant can be used to scan a program code and suggest a list of concepts that may be in the code, based upon its domain model knowledge. The computational approach is a connectionist-based inference engine (TAO). The domain model (DM) is a network in which each concept is represented as a node and the relationships between nodes are represented as arcs.

We evaluate Biggerstaff's work based on the technical issues discussed in Chap. 1 as follows.

- **Extent:** The papers indicate that applications with multiple source files are analyzed.

- **Ordering:** It is conceivable that logic rules could in some instances recognize different orderings of operands and statements as being equivalent. No discussion of this problem is found in the papers.

- **Variation:** There is no indication in the papers that there is any provision made for variation in the source text, beyond alternate spellings of procedure and data structure variable names. The fact that the spelling of procedure and variable names is used in the analysis limits the variation to programmers who think in the same language as the implementors of this system.

- **Focus:** This is an interactive system. The authors don't mention any automatic focus mechanism.

- **Non-contiguousness:** It is conceivable that logic rules could in some instances recognize logically related program elements that are not lexically adjacent. No discussion of this problem is found in the papers.

- **Selection:** Like all display-oriented projects, DESIRE does not have to handle the selection problem.

- **Correctness:** Like all display-oriented projects, DESIRE does not have to handle the correctness problem.

- **Scalability:** There is no discussion of the complexity of the analysis methods.

Kozaczynski and Ning's Concept Recognizer

The purpose of Kozaczynski and Ning's work (31) (32) is to enable programmers to understand what an existing program does so that they can perform such tasks as enhancement, debugging, and migration. For these purposes, this work seeks to identify abstract concepts in code.

Their knowledge base is structured as a hierarchy of concept classes. The specification of how to recognize an abstract concept contains information about the components (subconcepts) of the concept and constraints among the sub-concepts. These specifications, or plans, are compared to the code by checking the structural equivalence of the plan **abstract syntax tree** (AST) and the candidate AST. If a match occurs, the plan attributes are instantiated.

Both the structure and the constraints of the plan and candidate must match. Plans are patterns. Patterns contain constant nodes, which must match exactly, and pattern variables, which match arbitrary objects. If this match succeeds, then the constraints between sub-concepts are checked.

A parser creates abstract syntax trees from source code. These AST's are then augmented with the following information: a control flow graph, call relationships, data flow definition-use chains, and control flow domination and control dependence relations.

Concept recognition is a top-down process applied to the augmented AST's. Each time the system attempts to recognize a concept, it iterates over all the permutations of the sub-concepts of the plan. For each permutation, it evaluates the concept constraints. Permutations of sub-concepts must have a consistent binding of variables to elements of the pattern.

Since exhaustive enumeration approach is expensive, constraints are evaluated as permutations are generated, rather than after the whole set is completed. The search space is also pruned with several heuristics. The sets of sub-concepts that are most likely to fail are evaluated earlier, as are the smaller sets of sub-concepts.

We evaluate Kozaczynski and Ning's work based on the technical issues discussed in Chap. 1 as follows.

- **Extent:** The tool processes applications containing multiple procedures.

- **Ordering:** The papers do not mention this problem or a solution.

- **Variation:** The papers do not mention this problem. They could conceivably deal with some variation by putting duplicate entries in their knowledge base, at the cost of additional processing.

- **Focus:** This is an interactive system. The papers don't mention any automatic focus mechanism. The user can ask for all concepts to be recognized, or for the system to recognize only selected plans.

- **Non-contiguousness:** The Concept Recognizer deals with this problem by exhaustive search of permutations of sub-concept instances, augmented with heuristics that evaluate constraints as permutation is done.

- **Selection:** Like all display-oriented projects, Concept Recognizer does not have to handle the selection problem.

- **Correctness:** Like all display-oriented projects, Concept Recognizer does not have to handle the correctness problem.

- **Scalability:** The component of the system that dominates the performance of concept recognition is "the permutation over sub-concept instance sets." The authors characterize the complexity of this operation as follows: for all plans to match against the program, for all sub-concepts in the plan, compute the product of the number of instances in the program that match that sub-concept.

Kozaczynski and Ning consider the performance of their Concept Recognizer system "poor," even processing small COBOL programs of a few hundred lines. They do not believe that the performance could be seriously improved, "due to the inherent complexity of the pattern-matching problem."

The experience of the users of Kozaczynski and Ning's system is typical of the difficulties inherent in rule-based systems. (32).

"During the experiment we found that the users could not use the concept recognition tool effectively by themselves because they had difficulties in understanding the syntax and semantics of the plan language."

Quilici's DECODE

The purpose of Quilici's work (44) (43) (8) is to automatically extract object-oriented design knowledge to assist in translating C programs to C++.

The approach is similar to Kozaczynski and Ning's work. It begins with their plan representation and adds features to improve efficiency. Each plan also has an index that specifies when it should be considered. If the specified component appears in the program and the constraints are satisfied, then the plan should be considered.

Another extension Quilici added is that a plan can conditionally imply other plans. If the right extra components exist and additional constraints are true, then it attempts to match a modified or extended version of the plan.

Instead of working top-down, DECODE's matching algorithm works bottom-up. It is code-driven rather than library-driven. The algorithm walks the abstract syntax tree. When it finds a component that is an index for a plan, if the indexing constraints are true, it attempts to match the remaining components of the plan against the code. If a plan is recognized, and if it implies another plan, the algorithm attempts to match the implied plan. For all the recognized plans, it recursively checks for indexes to other plans.

We evaluate Quilici's work based on the technical issues discussed in Chap. 1 as follows.

- **Extent:** The extent of analysis seems to be a single procedure. It is not explicitly stated.

- **Ordering:** A special pass is made over the abstract syntax tree produced by the parser to rewrite various surface level sources of ordering differences into a canonical form.

- **Variation:** A special pass is made over the abstract syntax tree produced by the parser to rewrite various surface level sources of variation into a canonical form.

- **Focus:** This is an interactive system. We were unable to identify any discussion of automatic focus in the papers.

- **Non-contiguousness:** The use of a syntax tree for representing the user program, and the bottom-up matching of the tree with plans, mean that there is no provision for discovering related items that are not a part of the same programming language construct.

- **Selection:** Like all display-oriented projects, DECODE does not have to handle the selection problem.

- **Correctness:** Like all display-oriented projects, DECODE does not have to handle the correctness problem.

- **Scalability:** We were unable to identify any discussion of the complexity of the algorithms employed. The bottom-up approach with plan indexing will cause the CPU time required to grow more slowly than some of the other approaches in the Program Understanding camp.

Woods, Quilici, and Yang's MAP-CSP

The most recent work in the display-oriented projects is also the most comprehensive (57). The authors are interested in the problem of "program understanding", which they define as "the formation of an abstract, conceptual description" of the set of instructions in a program. They characterize the previous work in this field as plan-based program understanding, which they divide into two camps: Abstract Syntax Tree based approaches (Kozaczynski and Ning, (32) Quilici (8)) and Graph based approaches (Wills, (53) Hartman (24)). Their assessment is "despite some promising program understanding research efforts, there has so far been no clear evidence that these approaches scale to the size of real-world software systems."

Their work is based on the hypothesis that they can "build upon the standard method of structural analyses by also automating part of the conceptual understanding process" by doing the following.

1) Identifying design concepts at various levels of abstraction.

2) Representing the implementations of these design concepts as collections of code entities or design concepts and relationships between them that implement the design concept.

3) Implementing an efficient algorithm for locating design concepts by finding code patterns in source program.

They see two parts of the program understanding problem:

Plan matching: Given a single plan, find all instances of the plan in the internal representation of the program.

Plan ordering: Given a hierarchically-organized plan library, determine the order of plans to try to find.

Their approach to the first part is to model it as a single Constraint Satisfaction Problem, which they refer to as *MAP-CSP*. Their approach to the second part is generating a sequence of Constraint Satisfaction Problems, which they call *Layered MAP-CSP*. There are many ways to solve such problems. Many involve backtracking search augmented with various heuristics to narrow down the possible search candidates. The algorithm works through the plan database from the bottom up. It starts by invoking the MAP-CSP analysis for each plan in the bottom layer, and then works through the higher layers.

The authors refer to a previous paper in which they proved that the computational task of recognizing a plan represented as a set of components and constraints is NP-hard. So, their hope is to find heuristics that reduce the actual computation involved. They believe that this is reasonable since "there are many other problems that are NP-hard in general for which there are CSP-solving strategies that prove to be effective in practice."

They characterize the size of an unconstrained search space for a single MAP-CSP problem as "bounded by M^N (where N is the number of components in a plan and M is the size of the source) and N is fixed for any given plan matching problem. The result is a search space that is polynomial in N."

They present lots of experimental data for solving the MAP-CSP problem using various heuristics. Unfortunately, no complexity analysis of these heuristics are presented, so the experimental data is difficult to evaluate.

They feel that they can be optimistic about a viable implementation because "the problem is exponential in the plan size and not the program size." This only represents the complexity of a single application of MAP-CSP. They acknowledge that "the worst case complexity of Layered MAP-CSP is it $O(N * C - MAP - CSP)$, where it N is the number of plans in the library and C-MAP-CSP is the complexity of verifying whether there are instances of a hypothesized plan present." They imply that the value of N can be ignored because their Layered algorithm does not look at all plans in each layer. This is due to the fact that each component contains an index that points to all of the plans that contain it.

Based on their experimental data, they identified a number of defects in their heuristics. The most promising version of their system is a backtracking-based CSP solver that uses flow-relationships to identify new domain sets for the constraint variables. They consider this to be a hybrid of constraint satisfaction and graph-matching techniques.

We evaluate Woods, Quilici, and Yang's work based on the technical issues discussed in Chap. 1 as follows.

• **Extent:** The authors say that their current implementation does not compute data-flow relationships that cross function boundaries.

• **Ordering:** Brief mention is made of a special pass is made over the Abstract Syntax Tree produced by the parser to rewrite various surface level sources of ordering differences into a canonical form.

• **Variation:** Brief mention is made of a special pass is made over the Abstract Syntax Tree produced by the parser to rewrite various surface level sources of variation into a canonical form.

• **Focus:** We were unable to find a discussion of automatic focus in this work. The authors do not currently have an interactive implementation, but see benefit from having user guidance.

• **Non-contiguousness:** The use of a syntax tree for representing the user program, and the bottom-up assignment of abstract syntax tree elements to CSP variables, mean that there is no provision for discovering related items that are not a part of the same programming language construct.

• **Selection:** Like all display-oriented projects, MAP-CSP does not have to handle the selection problem.

• **Correctness:** Like all display-oriented projects, MAP-CSP does not have to handle the correctness problem.

• **Scalability:** The worst case time complexity for matching one single plan against a program is $M**N$, where N is the plan size and M is the program size.

The example of a tiny plan they present has six components, each of which is comprised of several underlying lexical elements in a corresponding program. Their bottom-level components in the example given correspond to simple C statements. Simple statements correspond roughly to non-comment source lines. This means that the complexity of matching the tiny plan of 6 components against a toy program of 100 lines is 100^6, (approximately 2^{40}) and the complexity of matching a plan of 10 components against a modest program of 1,000 lines is 1000^{10} (approximately 2^{100}).

Their experimental results suggest that, for some cases, the actual performance is not always as quite bad as the theoretical worst case. The bottom-up approach with plan indexing will cause the CPU time required to grow more slowly than some of the other approaches in the Program Understanding camp.

Program Understanding versus Algorithm Recognition

Our work is related to the display-motivated projects only in a very superficial sense. Most of these projects would classify themselves as being a part of the Program Understanding community. We find the following major differences between Program Understanding as they present it, and Algorithm Recognition as we define it.

The goal of Algorithm Recognition is fully automatic program optimization. Both semantic precision (Semantic Equivalence, Def. 2.2) in the recognition process and semantic correctness in the replacement process are a must.

The goal of the Program Understanding projects is design concept recovery. Semantics precision is neither required nor guaranteed, because program understanding is partially automated, interactive, or human-assisted.

Algorithm Recognition has formal, exact, and mathematically rigorous definitions of Algorithmic Equivalence (Def. 2.3) and Algorithmic Instance (Def. 2.7).

There is not yet any formal or exact definition of Plan Recognition. Their definition, if any, is given in terms of their solution methods, such as constraint satisfaction or graph parsing.

The technical approach for Algorithm Recognition is tree matching.

The technical approaches for Program Understanding follow a rule based derivation process, or inverse of the derivation process, such as graph parsing or constraint satisfaction.

The internal representation of programs and patterns for Algorithm Recognition are the same. The control tree captures the control flow information of the program. Besides the arcs of the tree, there are other arcs in our internal representation which capture the data flow information as well as dependence information. The dependence information is a result of dependence testing of array subscripts, which is fundamental to loop transformations used for vectorization, parallelization, and memory hierarchy optimizations used for high performance computing systems.

In Algorithm Recognition, patterns are organized in a database which is indexed by invariants.

There is some similarity between our control-tree and the abstract syntax tree used by the Program Understanding projects. Our control-tree can not be generated simply from a parser though. For example, the control nodes are the results of deep semantic analysis.

The internal representations of programs and patterns for Program Understanding are different. In some projects, programs are represented as AST's or a parse tree with added data flow information. In other projects they are represented with graphs. In some projects, plans or templates are represented as annotated graphs and in others, special pattern-based language rules are used.

In Program Understanding, some projects organize plans as a flat list, while others have a hierarchical structure, in which a plan can have other plans as subplan.

In Algorithm Recognition, a pattern is a subprogram (Def. 2.1), which is just a list of program statements. For example, variables in our pattern are regular program variables.

In Program Understanding a plan corresponds to an abstract description that captures the crucial details of one possible implementation of a design concept. There no formal and exact definition of a plan. There are just examples. For example, a variable in their pattern corresponds to a design concept. This may not be related to any variable in the program.

In Algorithm Recognition, pattern matching is testing the existence of a binary relation (Algorithmic Instance, Def. 2.7) between two subprograms (Def. 2.1).

In Program Understanding, plan matching is the process of starting with a single plan, and finding all instances of the plan in the internal representation of the program. There is no formal and exact definition of the "instance".

3.3   Replacement-Motivated Projects

Snyder's Idiom Optimization proposal

The purpose of Snyder's work (47) is to recognize the idioms in an arithmetic expression and to select a non-overlapping subset of the recognized idioms that maximizes the benefit of optimizations. His approach is different from the other replacement-oriented efforts in that the operands of an operator in an idiom may not only match constants and variables, but also arbitrary expressions.

Snyder presents an algorithm for recognizing idioms whose complexity is $O(n \log n)$, where n is the size of the expression tree. This bound assumes that the size of the idiom set is a constant, relative to the size of the expression and can be ignored.

Idioms can overlap in a parse tree. Snyder presents a **dynamic programming** algorithm that selects a non-overlapping subset of recognized idioms of a parse tree that maximizes the benefit of optimization.

We evaluate Snyder's work based on the technical issues discussed in Chap. 1 as follows.

- **Extent:** This proposal works only on expressions.

- **Ordering:** This proposal does handle permutation of the operands of commutative operators, which is the only source of ordering problems in an expression.

- **Variation:** Many of the sources of program variation do not occur within the extent of this proposal, which only covers a single expression.

- **Focus:** Snyder's work does not discuss how he would focus on the most important expressions.

- **Non-contiguousness:** Snyder's work is limited to expressions and idioms recognized must be contiguous sub-trees of an expression tree.

- **Selection:** Selection is done with a dynamic programming algorithm.

- **Correctness:** The issue of the correctness of replacing multiple statements was not a concern for Snyder, who dealt only with single expressions.

- **Scalability:** Snyder summarizes the scalability problems with his approach as follows:

"our complexity bounds for the algorithms are derived on the assumption that the input expression grows without bound, and thus the size of the idiom set can be ignored. In a sense we are 'matching the idioms to the expression.' But what if the idiom set is large compared to a typical expression? Then we might wish to 'match the expression to the idioms.' This suggests that better algorithms are possible and that preprocessing of the idioms might be useful. "

Even the smallest set of APL idioms contains at least 100 items. The typical APL expression contains 10 or fewer nodes in a tree representation. This means that a minimal idiom set is an order of magnitude bigger than a typical expression. So, his complexity bounds aren't valid, and his approach isn't scalable for the application he has targeted.

Pinter and Pinter's Loop Optimization proposal

The purpose of Pinter and Pinter's work (40) is to propose a method for recognizing parallelizable idioms in scientific programs. Their particular focus is on idioms that contain recurrences of the sort that prevent automatic vectorization.

The application domain that this work addresses is scientific programs that can use data parallelism. The approach assumes that standard basic block optimizations, as well as vectorizing loop transformations have been performed before idiom optimization begins. It is intended to be complementary to existing vectorization techniques.

The chief contribution of this work is the definition of a **computation graph**, which is a modified extension of the program dependence graph (18). This graph represents loop nests. It is created by working from the inner-most loop in a nest outwards. A loop is unrolled so that each of its loop carried dependencies are between two consecutive iterations. The graph of the loop is replicated three times, representing the "initial," "middle," and "final" iterations. These are fused into the computation graph. The benefit of doing this is removing cycles in the data flow dependence graph.

Once the graph is constructed, the approach matches and replaces patterns by using a graph grammar to describe rewrite rules. This process continues until there are no more applicable changes.

We evaluate Pinter and Pinter's work based on the technical issues discussed in Chap. 1 as follows.

- **Extent:** This proposal targets nested loops.

- **Ordering:** The authors do not discuss this issue. There is no indication that their system does anything to deal with the problem.

- **Variation:** This system presupposes that a vectorizing compiler has already processed their input first. They do not address the issue of variation. but the side effect of their approach is that some sources of variation will be eliminated by the scalar and loop transformations that such a compiler must perform to be effective.

- **Focus:** The issue of focus is not discussed explicitly. The inference one can draw from the paper is that they intend to process all loops that were not vectorized by traditional data dependence analysis and loop transformations.

- **Non-contiguousness:** This system relies on a graph representation, the Program Dependence Graph. This will connect program elements that are related by data or control flow, but are not lexically contiguous.

- **Selection:** The authors explain the problem of the selection of optimization rules to apply when there are multiple choices in terms of rule ordering.

"In general, the order in which rules are applied and the termination condition depend on the rule set. If the rules are Church-Rosser then this is immaterial, but often they are competing (in the sense that the application of one would outrule the consequent application of the other) or are contradictory (creating potential oscillation). This issue is beyond the scope of this paper ... "

- **Correctness:** This work does not address the issue of the correctness of replacing multiple statements.

- **Scalability:** In theory, this proposal has the same scalability problems as others that use parsing with graph grammars. In practice, the scalability limitations will be somewhat less since the extent of the analysis is limited to individual loop nests. There is no discussion of scalability in the paper.

This work does not handle indirect array references, such as $A(P(I))$. This is a serious deficiency, since the clear trend in numerical applications is to use sparse and non-rectangular data structures. Indirect array references are the most common way to implement these structures in Fortran.

Kessler's PARAMAT

There are several purposes of Kessler's work (27) (28) (29). The goal of the pattern recognizer is to annotate nodes in an abstract syntax tree with a "pattern instance." This is a structure that describes the function computed at the subtree rooted at that node, along with the parameters of that function. Depending on the target architecture, this information will be used to perform automatic parallelization of loops, to perform automatic data distribution of data structures, and to replace code with calls to library procedures.

The PARAMAT system begins with a preprocessing phase. This phase substitutes procedure bodies for procedure calls, propagates constants, recognizes induction variables, and eliminates dead code.

Pattern recognition is a postorder traversal of the AST from left to right. Leaf nodes are recognized directly. Interior nodes are tested by calling a C function, a "template realization." This procedure tests the patterns matched by the children of the node. It determines whether the computation rooted at the node is the operation being matched. If the test succeeds, the procedure maps the elements of the AST to the pattern parameters, and annotates the node with name of the matched pattern.

When the interior node is a loop header, the system performs loop distribution and scalar expansion on the loop before testing it. Data dependence analysis information is computed incrementally as needed. The recognition process visits each distributed loop separately.

Patterns are organized in a pattern hierarchy graph (PHG). For each pattern, there can be several template realizations. One pattern can be a "trigger" of another. Trigger relationships connect the elements of the PHG. The selection of which template realizations to compare against a given node is determined by which of its children is a trigger.

Related computations that are textually separated can be recognized as a part of a single pattern by including "cross edges" in the pattern. These are intended to represent loop-independent data flow relations.

We evaluate Kessler's work based on the technical issues discussed in Chap. 1 as follows.

- **Extent:** PARAMAT deals with whole programs by substituting called procedures inline.

- **Ordering:** PARAMAT stores some patterns containing varying orders (typically one to three) that have been encountered in practice. This is efficient, but will miss any orderings not stored in the database.

- **Variation:** PARAMAT reduces some types of variation with preprocessing by compiler transformations. It appears that the choice of transformations for this stage is due to the fact that they don't require data dependence analysis. Other variation is reduced during the matching process, with transformations that do require this analysis, such as loop distribution. Some variation, such as loop unrolling, is handled with special pattern features.

- **Focus:** The system naturally operates on loop nests. We were unable to identify in Kessler's papers any discussion of the problem of determining which loop nests are most important to optimize.

- **Non-contiguousness:** The author adds special information (cross-edges) to his patterns to connect non-contiguous but related elements. He adds these manually when he observes their occurrence in example codes.

- **Selection:** The bottom-up traversal performing both recognition and replacement means that the first pattern that matches a subtree will cause its replacement. It also means that a sub-optimal replacement can easily be selected.

- **Correctness:** Although PARAMAT performs replacements, we were unable to identify any discussion of the problem of performing correct replacements of multiple statements in his papers.

- **Scalability:** The system visits each node only once, and the processing time is said to be dominated by the linear tree traversal. This would indicate that it should scale better than most of the efforts surveyed here. There is no explicit discussion of complexity in Kessler's papers.

Bhansali and Hagemeister's proposal

The purpose of Bhansali and Hagemeister's work (3) (4) is to analyze the semantics of a program in terms of domain-specific concepts. While the goal is replacement, the proposed system will be interactive. The system will identify potential parallel code segments, while the user is responsible for selecting the parallelism and performing the replacement.

This effort organizes its database in terms of base, intermediate, and domain concept patterns. Base patterns are related directly to the code being analyzed. Domain patterns are related to application areas.

Analysis begins with the user telling the system the potential application domains that the code could represent. This information is used to derive a set of base concept patterns from the domain concept patterns. The abstract syntax tree of the code being analyzed is searched for these base patterns. When base patterns are recognized, they can lead to recognition of intermediate and domain concept patterns.

The rules of the pattern language include basic Fortran constructs and pattern symbols. The latter can match any code fragment of the appropriate type. These can be named so that values may be bound to them for future reference.

We evaluate Bhansali and Hagemeister's work based on the technical issues discussed in Chap. 1 as follows.

- **Extent:** The pattern language described is limited to describing a single subroutine. The representation of the user program is based upon an abstract syntax tree generated by a parser. Thus the extent of analysis is a single procedure as originally written by the programmer, with no analysis across procedure calls.

- **Ordering:** No compiler transformations, or special techniques or representations are employed to deal with the problems of multiple valid orderings.

- **Variation:** No compiler transformations, or special techniques or representations are employed to reduce program variation as written by the original programmer.

- **Focus:** The user must tell the system which application domains the code contains. The system generates a list of base concepts from the list of domains. It will only process syntax trees that contain those concepts. There is no automatic focus mechanism.

- **Non-contiguousness:** The use of a syntax tree for representing the user program, and the bottom-up decoration of the tree with identified concepts, mean that there is no provision for discovering related items that are not a part of the same programming language construct.

- **Selection:** Although the authors target their work to ultimately perform replacements, we were unable to identify any discussion of the problem of selecting the best replacements in their work.

- **Correctness:** Although the authors target their work to ultimately perform replacements, they currently leave the burden of assessing the correctness of a replacement, and performing that replacement, to the user.

- **Scalability:** The authors indicate that their approach is similar to a re-engineering tool that "does not scale up to our problem of matching patterns in a potentially large pattern library." They explain some of the techniques their approach would use to mitigate this problem, but do not present enough details of their pattern matching algorithm to assess its scalability.

diMartino and Iannello's PAP Recognizer

There are several purposes of diMartino and Iannello's work (14) (15). They seek to recognize concept instances in applications in order to perform semantic analysis. Their papers discuss the usefulness of this information for selecting an appropriate parallel paradigm, for performing automatic data distribution, and for restructuring sequential code for parallelism with loop transformations or library calls. While the purposes of this work place it with the other replacement-motivated efforts, the results are currently displayed through a graphical browser. They are not actually used for automatic replacement.

The prototype system has been integrated into the Vienna Fortran Compilation System (59). This system is used to create a version of a program dependence graph (PDG), in which nodes are statements and edges are control and data dependencies. This representation is augmented with the following information:

- A link from the nodes back to the abstract syntax tree of the corresponding statement,
- Labels on control dependence edges indicating truth value,
- Labels on data dependence edges indicating variable name and dependence type,
- Control statements have an expression tree attached with the condition,
- Assignment statements have two expression trees attached with the right and left hand sides of the assignment,
- Additional nodes representing variable declarations and types.

Hierarchical concept recognition is performed by a sub-system written in Prolog. Plans for recognizing concepts are Prolog clauses. The head of the clause is the concept to be recognized. The body of the clause is contains terms representing the subconcepts that comprise the concept and constraints among those terms. Control and data dependence between nodes are tested by these constraints.

Recognition is performed in a top-down manner starting with the augmented PDG as a base. An hierarchical PDG (HPDG) is constructed as abstract concepts are recognized. Increasingly abstract concepts occur at higher levels of the hierarchy.

The backtracking feature of the recognition process makes it possible to handle some forms of syntactic variation not resolved by the PDG representation. It also allows the specification of one concept with multiple plans.

The global scope of visibility of the HPDG makes it possible to handle some forms of non-contiguous but related code not resolved by the HPDG representation. It also provides a means to address overlapping implementations of concepts.

We evaluate diMartino and Iannello's work based on the technical issues discussed in Chap. 1 as follows.

- **Extent:** We were unable to identify in the papers describing this work any discussion of the extent of the analysis. It would obviously be constrained by the features of the Vienna Fortran Compilation System (59) in which they have embedded their work. Analysis across procedure boundaries would be mandatory for this work to provide speedups in real applications, since their goal is automatic parallelization. Parallel speedups in real codes generally must include loop nests that contain procedure calls, in order to amortize the cost of parallelization and synchronization over a large body of computation.

- **Ordering:** The backtracking approach of the recognition process means that different orderings of operands and statements can be recognized. The search complexity grows exponentially with the code size, but the authors hope that the top-down approach they have taken will make the approach practical for real codes.

- **Variation:** The PAP Recognizer reduces some types of variation by converting programs to a Program Dependence Graph representation.

- **Focus:** This is the only effort to mention an explicit focusing method. They say that in the future they would like to investigate limiting the scope of analysis by using profile information.

- **Non-contiguousness:** The PAP Recognizer relies on a graph representation for programs to connect elements that are related by data or control flow, but are not lexically contiguous.

- **Selection:** Although the authors target their work to ultimately perform replacements, we were unable to identify any discussion of the problem of selecting the best replacements in their work.

- **Correctness:** Although the authors target their work to ultimately perform replacements, they currently leave the burden of assessing the correctness of a replacement, and performing that replacement, to the user.

- **Scalability:** The backtracking approach on a globally visible data structure, used by the PAP Recognizer, makes the search complexity grow exponentially with the size of the analyzed code. There is no explicit discussion of complexity.

3.4 Summary

We can summarize the state of research in this area as follows. The following issues have not been efficiently and comprehensively addressed by previous published work:

- extent of code analyzed, and
- ordering of operands and statements,

The following issues have been only partially addressed by previous published work:

- variation in the realization of an algorithm,
- non-contiguousness of logically related program elements,
- selection of alternative optimizations, and

The following issues have not been addressed by previous published work:

- focus on the important parts of the analyzed code,
- correctness of replacing multiple statements and maintaining parameter consistency, and
- scalability of the methods used.

Usability

All of the approaches reviewed in this section, except Biggerstaff's, work on the basis of a set of rules.

Some are *if-then* rules popular in artificial intelligence (AI) work. Others are rules that form a graph grammar or a tree grammar. There is a problem that is common to all rule-based approaches. Rule-based systems require an expert in the internal workings on the system to add recognition capability. Rules are hard to derive manually. None of the projects has suggested an automatic method for deriving them. We have already related our experience with this problem in the preface.

We consider this deficiency to be a fatal flaw in all the projects we have described. It makes them unusable as a basis for optimizing compiler products. *Our experience with pattern matching in production optimizing compilers is that the labor required to create patterns by hand makes such techniques unmaintainable on even a modest scale.* The experience of those who made their pattern notations accessible to users is that the users were largely unable to understand and manipulate the notation.

A final problem of the display-oriented approaches is that it is difficult to assess the quality of the output since the problem is so ill-defined. If two different abstractions are both discerned in the same program, who is to say which is correct?

Computational Complexity

There are two aspects of the question of computational complexity to consider. The first is the inherent difficulty of the problem being solved. The second is the time complexity of the proposed solution.

Previous replacement-motivated efforts do not characterize the difficulty of the problem they seek to solve. Instead, they only discuss the time complexity of their proposed or realized solutions.

In contrast, we characterize the complexity of the problem directly. While our work is definitely replacement-motivated, we formally define the problem we seek to solve. This makes it possible to provide a precise characterization of the inherent difficulty of the problem. In addition, we provide a comprehensive analysis of the time complexity of the individual parts of our approach, and of the approach as a whole.

The computational complexity of the various replacement efforts is very difficult to compare. The reason for this is that many of the efforts attempt to solve problems of widely varying extent. In addition, different efforts address some technical issues from Sect. 1.4 and ignore others. The time complexity of our approach is competitive with any of the previous efforts when only the same subset of technical issues is considered.

Several of the works suggest that the time complexity of their approach is bounded solely by some function of the number of rules in their database. They do not consider the size of the program being analyzed. We find their informal arguments unconvincing. A credible complexity analysis must consider both the size of input program being analyzed and the size of the knowledge database.

In the display-oriented projects, their approaches to plan recognition are usually based on some general purpose exhaustive search procedures. Heuristics are then used in organizing and selecting the plans in the recognition process. Generally speaking, efficient algorithms in any area of computation are designed by taking advantage of the special properties of the problems. The approaches of the display-oriented projects do not fully exploit the special properties of the application domain. These properties include programming language syntactic and semantic properties, and tree/graph algorithm properties. This is a major reason why they tend to be inefficient.

4 Reducing Program Variation

There are many ways that a given algorithm can be coded in a specific programming language. This phenomenon is called **program variation**. Our definition of algorithmic instance (Def. 2.7) does not cover all the possible variations, although the deficit could be made up by maintaining more algorithm patterns in the database. In this chapter, we discuss an approach to handle program variation.

4.1 Handling Program Variation

Wills (52) identifies seven sources of common program variations:

- Syntactic variation,
- Organization variation,
- Delocalization,
- Redundancy,
- Optimizations,
- Implementation variation, and
- Unrecognizable code.

We identify one more source of program variation – generalization.

Our approach to handling variation is to preprocess the computational kernel before pattern matching. We do this through a series of semantics-preserving transformations performed by an optimizing compiler. The transformations can help reduce the effect of these common sources of program variation.

Intermediate Representations

For the transformations, the computational kernel is represented in an intermediate form, the node graph. This graph contains both control flow and data flow dependence information, as used by the optimizing compiler back end. For pattern matching, the subprograms are represented by different forms, which will be discussed in detail in Chap. 5.

In the following sections, we explain each source of variation and give an example. We also discuss the compiler transformations that can be employed to reduce this variation, and give an example of their application.

4.2   Syntactic variation

In most high level languages, there is more than one way to express control flow and to bind values to names. A language with conditionals and gotos needs no looping constructs. A language that has variable assignment has no need of constructs for static initialization or named constants. Yet most high level languages contain all of these constructs. **Syntactic variation** occurs when the same algorithm is realized in different programs that use a different selection of control and **binding constructs** to achieve the same purpose.

Language Independent Representation

Trivial syntactic variations between languages include such things as the spelling of keywords or the location of punctuation. These can be eliminated by converting the parse trees generated during **syntactic analysis** to an intermediate representation suitable for representing multiple languages.

Control Flow Normalization

A **basic block** is a sequence of consecutive statements that has two properties. First, the sequence is always entered at the first statement and exited at the last statement. Second, if any statement in the sequence is executed, they are all executed. For the purposes of normalizing control flow, all control flow constructs should be resolved into conditional and unconditional jumps. **Control flow analysis** first groups statements into basic blocks. Then it discovers the looping structure of the procedure by analyzing a graph in which each basic block is a node.

After control analysis has uncovered the underlying structure, control flow can be reconstituted using higher level control constructs. This is **control flow normalization**. Figure 4.1 shows a code segment before and after control flow normalization is performed.

Control flow normalization alleviates the problem of syntactic variation. It reduces redundant control flow constructs to a small set of simpler constructs. Algorithms for performing control flow analysis can be found in (2, pp. 602–607) and (49, pp. 655–660).

Induction Variable Strength Reduction

Consider the code segments in Fig. 4.2. They are two different ways to express the same computation. In standard compiler optimization, the first will be converted into a form of the second through **induction variable strength reduction** (2, pp. 643–648). This optimization modifies the program to generate the same sequence of values for an induction variable, using a less costly set of instructions. For example, multiplications can often be replaced by additions.

```
      L = 1
      H = N
05  if( L .gt. H ) goto 40
      M = (L + H ) / 2
      if( A(M)- X ) 10,20,30
30    L = M + 1
      goto 05
10    H = M - 1
      goto 05
20    P =  M
      goto 40
40  return
```

```
      L = 1
      H = N
      do while (L .le. H )
        M = (L + H ) / 2
        if( A(M) .gt. X ) then
          L = M + 1
        else if ( A(M) .lt. X ) then
          H = M - 1
        else
          P =  M
          goto 10
        endif
      enddo
10  return
```

Figure 4.1
Control flow normalization — before and after

```
      do i = n,1,-1
        j = i * 4
        k = n - i  + 1
        A(i) = B(j) * C(k)
      enddo
```

```
      j = n * 4 + 4
      k = 0
      do i = n,1,-1
        j = j + -4
        k = k + 1
        A(i) = B(j) * C(k)
      enddo
```

Figure 4.2
Induction variable strength reduction — before and after

In our approach, we work with the concept of an induction value (Def. 2.4), which is more general than the concept of an induction variable. The process of turning the induction values to our internal representation (Sect. 5.4) includes the work of induction variable strength reduction.

4.3   Organization variation

The code in an application can be organized in many ways. For example, the statements can be grouped together as procedures in any order that preserves the intended semantics. The parameters of each procedure can be made available either as global variables or arguments. These parameters can be grouped into numerous combinations of individual values, flat aggregate structures, and recursive aggregate structures. The code in a single module can be organized into loop nests and conditional structures in a variety of ways. The local variables in a single module can be grouped into numerous combinations of individual values, flat aggregate structures, and recursive aggregate structures. **Organization variation** occurs when the same algorithm is realized in different programs that use a different partitioning or hierarchy of the statements or variables used in the computation.

Scalar Expansion

Scalar expansion replaces references to a scalar variable that occur in a loop with references to an array created by the compiler for this purpose, such that each iteration of the loop refers to a unique element of the array. Figure 4.3 shows a code segment before and after scalar expansion is performed.

```
do i = 1,n
  A = B(i) * C(i)
  D(i) = A * 2
  E(i) = A * (D(i) - 5)
enddo
```

```
do i = 1,n
  A$1(i) = B(i) * C(i)
  D(i) = A$1(i) * 2
  E(i) = A$1(i) * (D(i) - 5)
enddo
```

Figure 4.3
Scalar expansion — before and after

Scalar expansion reduces organization variation that arises from the programmer's choice of using scalar temporary variables or array elements. It always uses array elements where the transformation is appropriate. An algorithm for scalar expansion can be found in (58, pp. 225–228).

Reductive Scalar Temporary Removal

A **reduction** is an associative function applied pairwise to a set of values, resulting in a single value. Computing the sum or maximum value of a vector is a reduction.

Reductive scalar temporary removal identifies a reduction that has the following properties.

- The partial results of the reduction are stored in a scalar temporary.
- The initial value of the operation is copied from an array element to the scalar temporary.
- The result is copied back to that same element.

This optimization substitutes an array reference for the scalar temporary and removes the copy operations. The scalar variable is identified as a temporary variable because it has two properties. It is not used again, without an intervening assignment, and it is not an argument or global variable which would make its value available after the procedure finishes. Temporary scalars used in these reduction operations cannot be removed without the results of data dependence analysis. Figure 4.4 shows a code segment before and after reductive scalar temporary removal is performed.

Reductive scalar temporary removal reduces organization variation that arises from the programmer's choice of using scalar temporary variables or array elements to hold the results of reductions It always uses array elements where the transformation is appropriate.

Procedure Call Inlining

Procedure call inlining replaces a procedure call with a copy of the body of the called procedure. All references to the formal parameters of the called procedure are replaced with the actual arguments used at the call site. Figure 4.5 shows a code segment before and after procedure call inlining is performed.

Procedure inlining alleviates the problem of organization variation. It removes whatever procedure boundaries the programmer chose. The resulting code can suffer from a size explosion, if applied indiscriminately. This makes the technique counterproductive unless the inlining process is limited to the computational kernel of the application. This kernel can be identified by executing the application with instrumentation that creates an execution profile of the application.

```
do i = 1,n
  do j = 1,m
    T = C(i,j)
    do k = 1,p
      T = T + A(i,k) * B(k,j)
    enddo
    C(i,j) = T
  enddo
enddo
```

```
do i = 1,n
  do j = 1,m
    do k = 1,p
      C(i,j) = C(i,j) + A(i,k) * B(k,j)
    enddo
  enddo
enddo
```

Figure 4.4
Reductive scalar temporary removal — before and after

Loop Distribution

Loop distribution distributes a loop structure over each independent compound or simple statement in the loop body. Two statements can be placed in separate loop bodies if and only if they are not mutually data dependent. Fig(s). 4.6 and 4.7 show a code segment before and after loop distribution is performed.

For the purposes of reducing program variation, we use a variation on the standard loop distribution algorithm that performs as much distribution as possible. If this version were used for normal optimization purposes, however, it might not result in the best performance.

Loop distribution alleviates the problem of organization variation. It replaces the nest structure chosen by the programmer with one that separates unrelated computations into a maximal set of loops that preserve the semantics of the original program. An algorithm for loop distribution can be found in (58, pp. 197–205).

Conditional Distribution

Conditional distribution distributes a conditional structure over each independent compound or simple statement in the alternatives of a conditional statement. This transformation is often called **IF-conversion**. Figure 4.8 shows a code segment before and after conditional distribution is performed.

```
do i = 1,n
  do j = 1,m
    C(i,j) = DOT(A(i,1),n,B(1,j),1,p)
  enddo
enddo

real function DOT(X,INCX,Y,INCY,p)
DIMENSION X(*), Y(*)
DOT = 0.0
ix = 0
iy = 0
do k = 1,p
  ix = ix + INCX
  iy = iy + INCY
  DOT = DOT + X(IX) * Y(IY)
enddo
return
end
```

```
do i = 1,n
  do j = 1,m
    do k = 1,p
      C(i,j) = C(i,j) + A(i,k) * B(k,j)
    enddo
  enddo
enddo
```

Figure 4.5
Procedure call inlining — before and after

```
do i = 1,n
  do j = 1,m
    C(i,j) = 0.0
    F(i,j) = 0.0
    do k = 1,p
      C(i,j) = C(i,j) + A(i,k) * B(k,j)
      F(i,j) = F(i,j) + D(i,k) * E(k,j)
    enddo
  enddo
enddo
end
```

Figure 4.6
Loop distribution — before

Conditional distribution alleviates the problem of organization variation. It replaces the conditional structure chosen by the programmer with one that separates unrelated

```
do i = 1,n
  do j = 1,m
    C(i,j) = 0.0
  enddo
enddo
do i = 1,n
  do j = 1,m
    F(i,j) = 0.0
  enddo
enddo
do i = 1,n
  do j = 1,m
    do k = 1,p
      C(i,j) = C(i,j) + A(i,k) * B(k,j)
    enddo
  enddo
enddo
do i = 1,n
  do j = 1,m
    do k = 1,p
      F(i,j) = F(i,j) + D(i,k) * E(k,j)
    enddo
  enddo
enddo
```

Figure 4.7
Loop distribution — after

computations into a maximal set of guarded statements that preserve the semantics of the original program. An algorithm for IF-conversion can be found in (58, pp. 241–243).

Loop Permutation

Loop permutation reorders the loop structures of a nested loop while preserving the semantics of the original order.

For the purposes of reducing program variation, we use a variation on the standard loop permutation algorithm that selects an order based on the invariants of the graph representation of the enclosed loop body. If this version were used for normal optimization purposes, however, it might not result in the best performance.

Figure 4.9 shows a code segment before and after loop permutation is performed.

Loop permutation alleviates the problem of organization variation caused by arbitrary ordering. It creates a a canonical order for loops while preserving the semantics of the original program. When the order of loops is changed on a pairwise basis, it is called loop interchange. Tests for performing valid loop interchange can be found in (58, pp. 197–205).

```
if( X .eq. Y ) then
  A(i) = Q * 2
  B(i) = R * 3
  C(i) = S * 5
else
  D(i) = Q / 3
  E(i) = R / 5
endif
```

```
F = X .eq. Y
if( F ) then
  A(i) = Q * 2
endif
if( F ) then
  B(i) = R * 3
endif
if( F ) then
  C(i) = S * 5
endif
if( .NOT. F) then
  D(i) = Q / 3
endif
if( .NOT. F) then
  E(i) = R / 5
endif
```

Figure 4.8
Conditional distribution — before and after

```
do i = 1,n
  do j = 1,m
    do k = 1,p
      C(i,j) = C(i,j) + A(i,k) * B(k,j)
    enddo
  enddo
enddo
```

```
do j = 1,m
  do k = 1,p
    do i = 1,n
      C(i,j) = C(i,j) + A(i,k) * B(k,j)
    enddo
  enddo
enddo
```

Figure 4.9
Loop permutation — before and after

4.4   Redundancy

Redundancy causes program variation when the same algorithm is realized in different programs that recompute different quantities instead of storing and re-using the values.

Common Subexpression Elimination

An occurrence of an expression is a **common subexpression** if the expression was previously computed, and the values of the variables in the expression have not changed since the previous computation. **Common subexpression elimination** identifies parts of expressions that always compute the same value under the same conditions. It replaces all but one of the expressions with a reference to the location where the result of the one remaining expression is stored. This optimization may rearrange the structure of expressions in order to identify common components. Figure 4.10 shows a code segment before and after common subexpression elimination is performed.

```
if (K .lt. L ) then
  A = (C * 4) / -(J * B + sqrt(C))
else
  E = (E * 4) / -(J * B + sqrt(C))
endif
F = (B * 4) / -(J * B + sqrt(C))
```

```
T$1 =  -(J * B + sqrt(C))
if (K .lt. L ) then
  A = (C * 4) / T$1
else
  E = (E * 4) / T$1
endif
F = (B * 4) / T$1
```

Figure 4.10
Common subexpression elimination — before and after

Common subexpression elimination alleviates the problem of redundancy. It causes an expression to be evaluated once at the earliest point where it has the same meaning as in the original program text. Common subexpression elimination within a basic block provides no benefit in the context of our approach because we represent expressions as trees. Duplicate expressions must be represented separately, otherwise the tree becomes a graph. This transformation is useful to us within the context of a procedure, when assignments to temporary variables are introduced.

Common subexpression elimination within a basic block is typically performed by value numbering or converting a basic block to a directed acyclic graph (DAG). Algorithms for performing common subexpression elimination within a basic block can be found in (2, pp. 546–550), (49, pp. 620–631), and (38, pp. 379–381).

Algorithms for performing common subexpression elimination within a procedure can be found in (2, pp. 633–636) and (38, pp. 391–393).

Redundant Assignment Elimination

Redundant assignment elimination within a basic block removes all but the last of a sequence of assignments to a scalar variable that do not have an intervening use of the variable. Within a procedure, redundant assignment elimination removes assignments to scalar variables that do not have subsequent references in the procedure. Figure 4.11 shows a code segment before and after redundant assignment elimination is performed.

```
C X is a local variable, Y is a global variable
  if( A .GT. 0 ) then
    X = P * Q
    Y = P / Q
  else
    X = R + S
    Y = R - S
  endif
C X is not used after this point
```

```
  if( A .GT. 0 ) then
    Y = P / Q
  else
    Y = R - S
  endif
```

Figure 4.11
Redundant assignment elimination — before and after

Redundant assignment elimination alleviates the problem of redundancy caused by useless code. It removes statements that have no effect on the output of the program.

Unreachable Code Elimination

Unreachable code elimination identifies conditional tests whose result is computable at compile time and eliminates all the code that would be executed under a condition that never is true at run time. Figure 4.12 shows a code segment before and after unreachable code elimination is performed.

```
do i = 1,n
  if( .false. ) then
    A(i) = C(i) * D(i)
  else
    B(i) = C(i) / D(i)
  endif
enddo
```

```
do i = 1,n
  B(i) = C(i) / D(i)
enddo
```

Figure 4.12
Unreachable code elimination — before and after

Unreachable code elimination alleviates the problem of redundancy. It removes statements that have no effect on the output of the program. Programmers do not usually write code that offers opportunities for unreachable code elimination. They arise due to the following circumstances:

- Constant propagation and constant folding (see below) reduce comparisons and boolean expressions to boolean constants.
- **Macro substitution** evaluates boolean expressions to constants.

Loop Invariant Motion

Loop invariant motion identifies expressions that have the same value on every iteration of a loop and moves them to a place where they occur once, just before the loop is executed. In a nested loop, the expression may be moved out of more than one loop. Figure 4.13 shows a code segment before and after loop invariant motion is performed.

Loop invariant motion alleviates the problem of arbitrary ordering. It causes an expression to be evaluated at the earliest point where it has the same meaning as in the original program text. Algorithms for loop invariant motion can be found in (2, pp. 638–643), (49, pp. 637–646), and (38, pp. 398–399,404).

4.5   Optimizations

Optimizations cause program variation when the same algorithm is realized in different programs. The differences are due to changes made by the programmer to the the source code to reduce execution time or storage used when the program is run on a particular computer system.

```
do i = 1,100
  A = C / (E * B)
  X(i) = A + B + C
enddo
```

```
A = C / (E * B)
T$1 = A + B * C
do i = 1,100
  X(i) = T$1
enddo
```

Figure 4.13
Loop invariant motion — before and after

Loop Rerolling

Partial loop unrolling does the following to a loop:

- Replicate the loop body one or more times.
- Modify all references to the loop index variable in the copies of the loop body, so that they have offsets based on the number of the copy they are in.
- Modify the loop structure to reflect the number of iterations of the old loop that are performed in one iteration of the new loop.

Complete loop unrolling does the following to a loop:

- Replicate the loop body as many times as the loop will be executed. This must be computable at compile time.
- Replace all references to the loop index variable in the copies of the loop body, with a constant index which is based on the number of the copy they are in.

    Loop rerolling identifies both partially and completely unrolled loops and reverses these processes. Figure 4.14 shows a code segment before and after loop rerolling is performed.

    Loop rerolling alleviates the problem of manual optimizations. It ensures that all loops are represented in their most natural and compact form, without any unrolling.

Loop Distribution

Loop distribution is also performed to reverse the effects of manual or automatic loop fusion, and hence some refer to it as loop fission. **Loop fusion** combines the bodies of two adjacent loops that have the same iteration space, and do not have data dependencies that

```
do i = 1,n
  do j = 1,m
    do k = 1,p,4
      C(I,J) = C(I,J) + A(I,K)   * B(K,J)
                      + A(I,K+1) * B(K+1,J)
                      + A(I,K+2) * B(K+2,J)
                      + A(I,K+3) * B(K+3,J)
    enddo
  enddo
enddo
```

```
do i = 1,n
  do j = 1,m
    do k = 1,p
      C(I,J) = C(I,J) + A(I,K) * B(K,J)
    enddo
  enddo
enddo
```

Figure 4.14
Loop rerolling — before and after

prevent the transformation. When programmers do this manually, the normal motivation is to reduce the overhead of the loop increment, test, and branch.

4.6   Delocalization

In an algorithm, there can be expressions or statements that are independent of each other, and thus can be executed in an arbitrary order. In the source code, these statements can appear in an arbitrary order. Instead of using compiler transformations, we propose a more general and more powerful method (Chap. 6) to solve this source of program variation.

Sometimes, in a computational kernel, statements from two or more independent sections of code are intermingled. This makes it difficult to find sections of the computational kernel that can match the algorithm patterns. Once again, this is not easily solvable by compiler transformations. In Chap. 8, we will discuss in detail how to extract statements from the computational kernels that are more likely to match the algorithm patterns.

4.7   Implementation Variation

For any given abstract operation or data type, there are often multiple implementations. For example, a stack of integers can be implemented using an array or a linked list. **Implementation variation** occurs when the same algorithm is realized in different programs that use different concrete implementations for the same abstract operator or type. Semantic preserving transformations are of no help in reducing this type of variation. The different implementations must be stored separately in the knowledge base of programming constructs.

4.8   Unrecognizable Code

Unrecognizable code is the term Wills uses for code that is composed of patterns that are not in her knowledge base of programming techniques. This is really not a category of program variation, but rather a statement of the limitations of a particular approach. Semantic preserving transformations are of no help in dealing with this problem.

4.9   Generalization

There is one additional source of program variation that Wills did not recognize as such. This is the level of generalization of the source code. Several examples of generalization are listed below:

- A literal constant is replaced by a named constant or a variable that doesn't change value.
- A constant value is abstracted out as a formal parameter to a procedure.
- A constant value is decomposed into an expression that computes it.

Generalization causes program variation when the same algorithm is realized in different programs with different binding times for the same quantity. In practice, we find that library subroutines tend to have a higher level of generalization than the same code written for a single application.

Interaction with Pattern Matching

Unlike the transformations listed in the previous sections, there is a trade-off involved in performing the transformations that reduce variation due to generalization. If these transformations substitute constants for variable names or expressions that are not part of the definition of an i-val (Def. 2.4), they may prevent our approach from recognizing a pattern. See Chap. 2 for our definition of pattern matching (e.g., algorithmic instance testing).

On the other hand, if we do not have a pattern in our database that represents a partially generalized instance, these transformations may reduce the computational kernel to a version that is in the database. In order to recognize all generalizations of an algorithm, we might have to include a pattern for every partial evaluation of the most general form of the algorithm.

An Example

The upper part of Fig. 4.15 shows a well-known subroutine from the BLAS (Basic Linear Algebra Subroutine) library (17). The authors have gone to great effort to generalize it. Invocations on no operands (N=0) and invocations having no effect (A=0) are treated specially. The index increments (INCX,INCY) can be positive or negative integers, though the most typical invocation is with increments of one.

The lower part of Fig. 4.15 shows the same code segment after constant propagation, constant folding, and algebraic simplification have been applied to it, as well as unreachable code elimination. For this evaluation, we assume that constant propagation has provided non-zero values for N and A, and values of one for INCX and INCY.

Constant Propagation

Constant propagation identifies uses of scalar variables that always have the same constant value and replaces the use with the constant. Constant propagation can be performed within the scope of basic blocks, individual procedures, and an entire program.

Constant propagation alleviates the problem of manual generalization. It produces the simplest form of an expression that can be created with compile-time knowledge. Algorithms for performing constant propagation within a procedure can be found in (2, pp. 681–683), (49, pp. 679–680), and (38, pp. 364–367).

Constant Folding

Constant folding applies arithmetic and logical operations at compile time to expressions in which all operands are constants. Constant folding alleviates the problem of manual generalization. It produces the simplest form of an expression that can be created with compile-time knowledge. It is most useful in conjunction with algebraic simplification. Algorithms for performing constant folding can be found in (49, pp. 612–620) and (38, p. 330).

Programmers do not usually write code that offers opportunities for constant folding. They arise due to the following circumstances:

- Constant propagation substitutes constants for variables.
- Macro substitution evaluates expressions to constants.

```
subroutine saxpy (n, a, X,incx, Y,incy)
real X(*),Y(*)
if ( n .gt. 0 ) then
  if ( a .ne. 0.0 ) then
    if ( incx .eq. 1 .and. incy .eq. 1 ) then
      do i = 1, n
        Y(i) = a * X(i) + Y(i)
      end do
    else
      ix = 1
      iy = 1
      if ( incx .lt. 0 ) ix = 1 - (n-1) * incx
      if ( incy .lt. 0 ) iy = 1 - (n-1) * incy
      do i = 1, n
        Y(iy) = a * X(ix) + Y(iy)
        ix = ix + incx
        iy = iy + incy
      end do
    end if
  end if
end if
return
```

```
subroutine saxpy (n, a, X,incx, Y,incy)
real X(*),Y(*)
do i = 1, n
  Y(i) = a * X(i) + Y(i)
end do
return
```

Figure 4.15
Constant propagation — before and after

Algebraic Simplification

Algebraic simplification combines terms of expressions by applying various identity and inverse properties of arithmetic and logical functions. Algebraic simplification alleviates the problem of manual generalization. It produces the simplest form of an expression that can be created with compile-time knowledge.

Figure 4.16 lists the algebraic simplifications typically performed by an optimizing Fortran compiler.

Programmers do not usually write code that needs the trivial simplifications listed here. They arise due to the following circumstances:

- Constant propagation and folding reduce variables to constants.
- Macro substitution evaluates expressions to constants.

Expression	Result
X + 0	X
X * 1	X
X .AND. .TRUE.	X
X .OR. .FALSE.	X
X * 0	0
X .AND. .FALSE.	.FALSE.
X .OR. .TRUE.	.TRUE.
0 - X	-X
-1 * X	-X
X / -1	-X
X ** 0	1
1 ** X	1
X - X	0
X / X	1

Figure 4.16
Algebraic simplification

4.10   Summary

We apply standard optimizing compiler transformations to the computational kernel before attempting to perform algorithm recognition. This is our approach to the following sources of program variation:

- Syntactic variation,
- Organization variation,
- Redundancy,
- Manual optimizations, and
- Generalization.

Our approach to delocalization as a source of program variation depends on how it appears in the computational kernel. In Chap. 6, we present a method for dealing with arbitrary ordering of independent expressions or statements. In Chap. 8, we present a method for dealing with intermingled unrelated statements.

Our approach to implementation variation as a source of program variation is to store separate patterns in a database for each independent implementation.

5 Internal Program Representation

In this chapter, we explain the internal representation in our approach to an algorithm recognition and replacement system. We use the same representation for the original computational kernel, the algorithm pattern subprograms, and the subprograms extracted from the original program, called the extracted subprograms. A subprogram is represented jointly by several separate structures:

- the **control tree** represents the statements as well as the control structure of the subprogram,
- the **statement-level data flow dependence graphs**,
- the **type expressions**,
- the **i-val tree** representing the induction values, and
- the **parameter list**.

5.1   Representing Expressions

In our approach, we use a tree to represent an expression and/or assignment as follows.

- Operators ("add", "sub", "mul", "div", "abs", "exp", "max", "min", "mod", "eq", "ge", "gt", "ne", "not", "and", "eqv", "neqv", "or", "shift", "parentheses", "address", "convert") are represented by individual (internal) nodes, with the operands being their subtrees.
- Constants are represented by leaf nodes.
- A reference to an i-val is represented by a leaf node.
- A scalar variable is represented by a leaf node.
- A Fortran k-dimensional array element $V(E1, E2, ..., Ek)$ is represented by a subtree (see Fig. 5.1).

In Fig. 5.1, an array element $V(E1, E2, ..., Ek)$ is represented by a tree, where $T(E1)$, ..., $T(Ek)$ are the subtrees representing subscript expressions $E1$, ..., Ek, and "[ ]" is a special non-commutative operator.

For example, in the loop in Fig. 5.2, the assignment is represented as in Fig. 5.3.

Pointers And Arrays in C

As discussed in (26, pp. 93-122), C language pointers and arrays are closely related. In C, there are no multi-dimensional arrays; one-dimensional arrays are special pointers. A

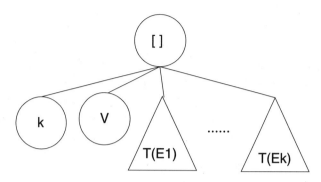

Figure 5.1
Representation of an array element

```
DO I = 1, n
   A(I) = X/Y - B(I)*(C(m+n)+Y+Z+5)
ENDDO
```

Figure 5.2
Assignment statement in loop

variable declared to be a pointer can be used as if it were an array, and vice versa. For example, the programs in Fig. 5.4 are two ways to do the same thing.

To avoid having to maintain too many algorithm patterns due to simple variations like this, C pointers and arrays are converted to a unified internal representation in our approach. For type expressions both array type and pointer type are converted to a form as shown in Fig. 2.4. For the variables in the statements, both arrays and pointers are converted to a form derived from address arithmetic. Both *p[15]* and **(p+15)* in the example above are represented as in Fig. 5.5, where the *?mem* variable introduced by the compiler represents the entire computer memory.

Our internal representation is still language independent, even though we represent Fortran array elements and C array elements in two different ways. The semantics of arrays are different in the two languages, so the representation must differ to some extent.

The semantics of a subtree rooted at a "[ ]" node is well defined. The language dependent part is the process that turns the source program into our internal representation.

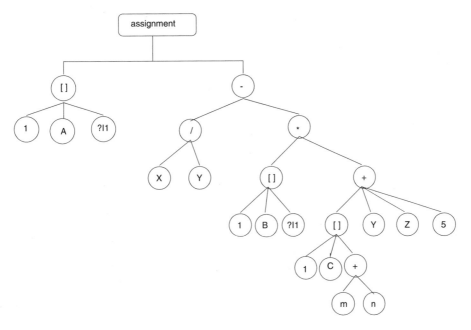

Figure 5.3
Representation of an assignment statement

```
main(){
  float *p = (float *) malloc(100 * sizeof(float));
  *(p+15) = 3.14;
  printf("\n  %f\n", p[15]);
}

main(){
  float p[100];
  p[15] = 3.14;
  printf("\n  %f\n", *(p+15));
}
```

Figure 5.4
Pointer and arrays are related in C

5.2   Representing Statements

Our approach handles C and Fortran programs written in certain styles. In our approach, the body of a program or a subprogram is represented by a tree consisting of various basic

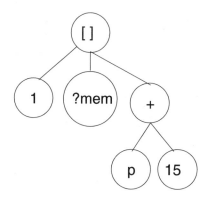

Figure 5.5
The internal representation of *p[15]* and **(p+15)* for C

constructs for its statements. This tree is called the **control tree**. It represents only the control flow structure of the program.

Data flow dependencies between the nodes of the control tree are represented by a separate graph. Its nodes are the leaves of the control tree that are variable references. Data flow dependencies include the following.

- A **true dependence** represents a DEF-USE relationship.
- An **anti dependence** represents a USE-DEF relationship.
- An **output dependence** represents a DEF-DEF relationship.

These three kinds of dependence constrain how statements can be reordered. (Refer to (58) for an exact definition of data flow dependence.) We will give examples to show both structures.

The basic constructs in the control tree are shown in Fig(s). 5.6, 5.7, 5.8, 5.9, 5.10, 5.11, 5.12, 5.13, 5.14, and 5.15. They also serve as a specification of the types of statements and the styles of the programs that our approach can handle. It handles programs written using the statements described below, plus any statements that can be converted by the preprocessor system to the following constructs. In other words, the design handles programs written in such styles that they can be represented internally in tree form. We shall see that they are more than the set of structured programs.

Figure 5.7 shows the construct related to the compound statement, such as the one in C. It is different because components of two different compound statements will be listed under the same control-group if they are all dominated by the same condition. The components of a compound statement may not be listed under the same control-group

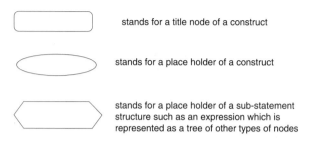

Figure 5.6
Notations used in the construct diagrams

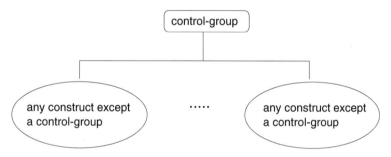

Figure 5.7
A **control-group** lists the statements executed under the same condition

if they are not dominated by the same condition. The statements listed under the same control-group are executed from left to right.

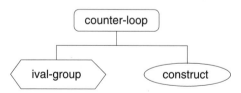

Figure 5.8
The **counter-loop** construct is used to represent Fortran **do** loops

Figure 5.8 shows the construct representing a loop for which the number of iterations is known when the loop begins execution. For example, a Fortran indexed, or counted *DO* loop belongs to this kind. For such a loop, there is at least one i-val, for the loop control variable. If this loop owns other i-vals, they also will be listed under the loop.

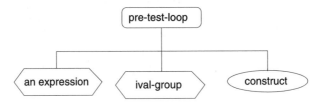

Figure 5.9
The **pre-test-loop** construct is used to represent C **while** loops

Figure 5.9 shows the construct representing a loop for which the number of iterations is unknown when the loop begins executing, and which is controlled by an expression that is tested every time before the loop body is executed. For such a loop, there can still be i-vals. If there is no i-val, the second child of the construct is a NULL pointer.

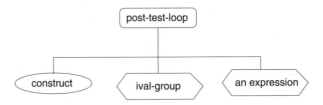

Figure 5.10
The **post-test-loop** construct is used to represent C **do-while** loops

Figure 5.10 shows the construct representing a loop for which the number of iterations is unknown when the loop begins executing, and which is controlled by an expression that is tested every time after the loop body is executed. For such a loop, there can still be i-vals. If there is no i-val, the second child of the construct is a NULL pointer.

Figures 5.11 and 5.12 show the two forms of conditional constructs supported. We do not have a construct just for representing the C *switch* or Fortran *computed goto* statements. If a computational kernel contains one of these statements that does not have any fall-throughs, then it may be decomposed into a series of conditional statements. For this to be possible, execution must continue immediately after the switch or computed goto statement. If a program contains one of these statements that do not fit this constraint, they induce a control flow graph that we cannot represent (see below).

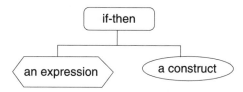

Figure 5.11
The **if-then** construct is used represent an **if-then** statement

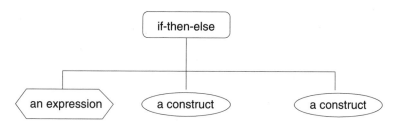

Figure 5.12
The **if-then-else** construct is used to represent an **if-then-else** statement

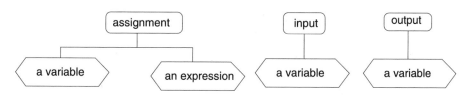

Figure 5.13
Constructs representing **Assignment** and **I/O** statements

Figure 5.13 shows the constructs to represent assignment, input, and output statements.

Figure 5.14 shows the constructs to represent a C *break* statement, a C *continue* statement, and a C *return* statement. If there is no returned value, the expression part is a NULL pointer. Although *goto* statements in general are not handled by our approach, we do accept a goto when its destination is the end of the enclosing loop body, the location immediately following the end of the enclosing loop, or the end of the subroutine/function. In other words, we accept a goto when it serves the purpose of a C continue, a C break, or a return statement. In this case, it will be represented internally using the *continue* construct, the *break* construct, or the *return* construct.

Figure 5.14
Constructs representing C **return**, **continue**, and **break** statements

The reason that we do not try to handle unrestricted *goto* statements is that we want to be able to represent the control flow structure of the program as a tree. Without this restriction, the control flow structure of the program has to be represented by an arbitrary **control flow graph**. Comparing the control flow graphs of two programs may require graph isomorphism testing, which has no known efficient algorithm. (Refer to Sect. 2.2.)

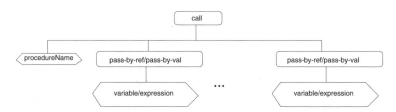

Figure 5.15
The **call** construct is used to represent a library procedure call

Figure 5.15 shows the construct to represent a procedure call after algorithm replacement. Procedure calls are no longer in the program representation after preprocessing to reduce program variation. They are, however, introduced by the algorithm replacement process. This construct is necessary to represent such a call.

Each specific library procedure call is represented by a customized construct. In the picture, *procedureName* node contains the name of the library procedure. The *pass-by-ref/pass-by-val* nodes represent two kinds of nodes: indicating the **parameter passing convention** for that particular argument, either pass by reference or pass by value.

5.3 Representing Type Expressions

Definition 2.5 defines the concept of type expression, which is used to describe the data type of a language construct. In our approach each type expression is represented as a tree. Figure 5.16 shows the basic constructs for the type expression tree.

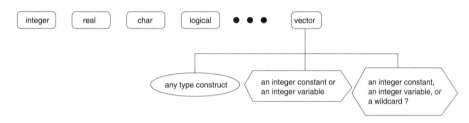

Figure 5.16
Type constructs

5.4 Representing Induction Values

We use a tree to represent an i-val. This representation will be used to match the i-vals of the pattern subprogram with the i-vals of the extracted subprogram. Let $?I:(begin, end, step)$ be an i-val, where $?I$ is the compiler generated identification of the i-val, and $begin$, end, and $step$ are expressions of free variables and other i-val identifications.

The term **free variable** here means that the variable can be substituted by an expression (e.g., more than just renaming). Definition 2.7 states the restrictions on variable renaming and substitution during algorithm pattern matching (algorithmic instance testing). We assume that the expressions are in a format as specified by the grammar in Fig. 5.17.

The i-val is represented by the tree shown in Fig. 5.18, where $T(begin)$, $T(end)$, and $T(step)$ are the parse trees of expressions $begin$, end, and $step$. These parse trees can be constructed in time complexity linear to the number of lexical tokens in $begin$, end, and $step$.

For example, consider i-val $?I2$: $(max(1, 1 - q), min(n, p - 1), 1)$, where p and q are free variables. The i-val is represented by the tree in Fig. 5.19. In implementation, the subtree representing an i-val can be in a simpler form.

Terminals:

- "+", "-", "*" – arithmetic operators,
- "var" – user created variable identification,
- "iv" – compiler generated i-val identification,
- "fe" – multilinear expressions of **free variables**, with integer coefficients,
- "min", "max", "mod", "div", "abs" – function names,
- "(" and ")".

Non-terminals:

- E – expression,
- V – multilinear expression of free variables,
- F – function, and
- I – expression of i-vals, not necessarily linear.

Rules:

```
E  ::  I | V | F | I+V | I+F | V+F | I+V+F
V  ::  fe
I  ::  T | T + I | T - I | iv * T | iv * T + I | iv * T - I
T  ::  var | var * T
F  ::  min(E,E) | max(E,E) | div(E,E) | mod(E, E) | abs(E)
```

Figure 5.17
The grammar for i-val representation

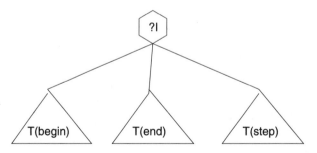

Figure 5.18
A subtree representing an i-val

5.5   Representing Parameters

For each pattern subprogram (refer to Def. 2.1 for this notation), a list of its parameters is maintained. Also recorded in the list is the information for each parameter indicating whether it is an input parameter, an input&output parameter, or an output parameter.

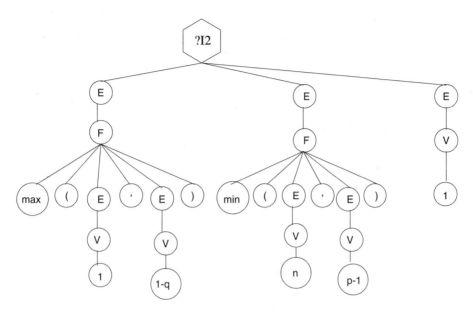

Figure 5.19
An i-val subtree

The order of parameters in this list is consistent with the order of the parameters of the corresponding library procedure. This consistency is important in determining the actual parameters for the library procedure call. This will be discussed in Chap. 11. Theoretically, we can think that the pattern subprogram and the corresponding library procedure have exactly the same parameters, listed in the same order.

5.6   Auxiliary Data Structures

Statement-Level Data Flow Dependence Graphs

In our control tree representation, each control-group node is associated with a statement-level data flow dependence graph. The vertices of this graph are the children (as statements) of the control-group node. There are three types of arcs.

- If the value of a variable defined in S_1 is referenced in S_2, then there is a **true dependence** arc from statement S_1 to statement S_2.

- If a variable is referenced in S_1 before it is defined in S_2, and if there is no assignment to that variable in between S_1 and S_2, then there is an **anti dependence** arc from S_1 to S_2.

- If S_1 defines a a variable and, before the value is referenced, S_2 defines the variable again, then there is an **output dependence** from S_1 to S_2.

The statement-level data flow dependence graphs can be constructed from the variable-level data flow dependence graphs. These can produced by an optimizing compiler used as a preprocessor.

Variable-Level Data Flow Dependence Graphs

For the computational kernel or an algorithm pattern P, its **variable-level data flow dependence** graph is a directed graph whose vertices are the occurrences of the variables in P. An occurrence of a variable represents either a definition or a reference to the variable. There are three types of arcs.

- If the value defined at d is referenced at r, then there is a **true dependence** arc from occurrence d to occurrence r.

- If there can be an execution of the subprogram in which a variable is referenced at r before it is defined at d, and there is no assignment to the variable in between r and d during the execution, then there is an **anti dependence** arc from r to d.

- If there can be an execution of the subprogram in which a variable is defined at d_1 and, before it is referenced, defined again at d_2, then (d_1, d_2) is an **output dependence** arc in the graph.

The general idea of how to construct the statement-level data flow dependence graphs from the variable-level data flow dependence graphs is as follows. Let T be a control tree for a subprogram whose variable-level data flow dependence graph is given. Let CN be a control-group node on T with children v_1, v_2, ..., v_k. For $1 \leq i \neq j \leq k$, (v_i, v_j) is an arc in the statement-level data flow dependence graph if and only if there is a data flow dependence arc in the variable-level data flow dependence graph from a leaf in $subtree(v_i)$ to a leaf in $subtree(v_j)$, where $subtree(v_i)$ is the subtree (of T) rooted at v_i, as shown in Fig. 5.20.

All the statement-level data flow dependence graphs can be constructed simultaneously by going through all the arcs of the variable-level data flow dependence graph. In particular, we compute the **lowest common ancestor** of the end points of each arc of the variable-level data flow dependence graph. If that ancestor is a control-group node, we make an arc linking two of its children. Using the algorithms in (23) and (51), T can be preprocessed in $O(|T|)$ time. After preprocessing, the lowest common ancestor of any pair of nodes can be computed in $O(1)$ time. Therefore, given the variable-level data flow dependence graph for the computational kernel with control tree T, its statement-level data flow dependence graphs can be constructed in $O(|T|)$ time.

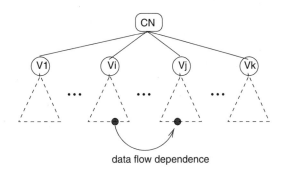

data flow dependence

Figure 5.20
Constructing the statement-level data flow dependence graphs

In our approach, only statement-level data flow dependence graphs are maintained. The variable-level data flow dependence graph is no longer needed once the statement-level data flow dependence graphs are constructed.

5.7   Examples

Consider the Fortran version of matrix multiplication in Fig. 5.21.

```
subroutine MM(A,B,C,m,n,p)
  integer m,n,p
  double precision A(m,n), B(n,p), C(m,p)
  integer i, j, k
  do i = 1, m
    do j = 1, p
      C(i,j) = 0
    enddo
  enddo
  do i = 1, m
    do j = 1, p
      do k = 1, n
        C(i,j) = C(i,j) + A(i,k)*B(k,j)
      enddo
    enddo
  enddo
  return
end
```

Figure 5.21
Matrix multiply example

```
function BSch(x,A,n)
integer n, L, H
real A(n), x
BSch = 0
L = 1
H = n
do while (L .LE. H)
   M = (L+H)/2
   if (A(M) .GT. x) then
      L = M+1
   else if (A(M) .LT. x) then
      H = M-1
   else
      BSch = M
      goto 10
   endif
enddo
10    return
end
```

Figure 5.22
Binary search example

The control tree of this subroutine is shown in Fig. 5.23. Siblings in the tree are listed top-down. The nodes of the data flow graph are the variable leaves of the control tree. The highlighted nodes indicate that a variable is defined at that point. Non-highlighted nodes indicate that a variable is referenced at that point. For visual clarity, we duplicate these leaves and draw them at the same horizontal levels as the originals. The arcs in the data flow graphs are tagged, near their sources, with "A" (anti-dependence), "T" (true-dependence), or "O" (output dependence).

Consider the Fortran version of a binary search in Fig. 5.22.

The control tree of this subprogram is shown in Fig. 5.24. It is drawn using the same conventions as Fig. 5.23.

5.8   Remarks

Type *struct* in C

We propose to use an existing compiler system as a preprocessor for an algorithm recognition and replacement system. In this compiler, a member of a *struct* data type is treated as an independent variable by itself. For example, the declaration *struct int k*; *char * pv*; introduces two variables. The first is named $v.k$ and has integer type. The second is named $v.p$ and has pointer to char type. This scheme prevents us from considering recursive types

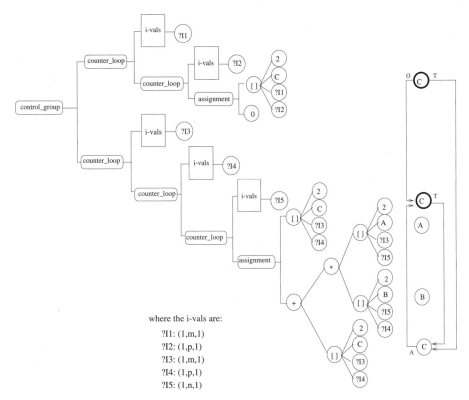

where the i-vals are:

?I1: (1,m,1)
?I2: (1,p,1)
?I3: (1,m,1)
?I4: (1,p,1)
?I5: (1,n,1)

Figure 5.23
The control tree and the variable-level data flow dependence graph for a matrix multiply subroutine

such as a pointer to structure used in a linked list. Fortunately, linked lists are seldom used in numerical computations, the primary application area we have targeted.

The Size of the Internal Representation

For our purposes, we will define the size of a source program to be the number of lexical tokens in the program. The size of the control tree, in number of nodes, is about the same as the size of the source program. This can easily be seen by reviewing the constructs we use to represent statements and expressions. The size of the subtree representing an i-val is no more than four times the number of lexical tokens in the induction values of the source program. This can be seen by reviewing the grammar in Fig. 5.17. The number of nodes in the variable-level data flow dependence graph is the same as the number of occurrences of the variables in the source program. The number of nodes in a statement-level data flow

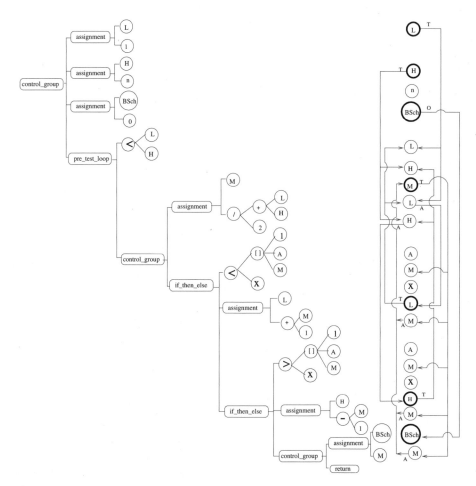

Figure 5.24
The control tree and the variable-level data flow dependence graph for a binary search function

dependence graph is the same as the number of children of the corresponding control-group
node. In the following chapters, we will discuss the time complexities of the algorithms in
terms of these sizes.

5.9   Summary

- We use trees to represent the following major components:
    - –Expressions and assignments
    - –Control flow constructs
    - –Type expressions
    - –Parameter lists
    - –Induction values
- We construct a statement-level data flow dependence graph from the variable level data flow dependence graph.
- Our representation handles programs written in such styles that they can be represented internally in tree form.

6 Converting to a Canonical Form

6.1 Expression Trees

Checking whether a subprogram is an algorithmic instance of one of the pattern subprograms in the database is not only difficult (see Thm. 2.3) but also time consuming. In our approach, the subprograms are compared based on the internal representation, mainly the control tree and the list of i-vals. To find an efficient solution to this problem, our approach is to convert the control trees into a canonical form, and to list the i-vals in a canonical order. The advantages of this approach include the following:

- The patterns can be preprocessed off-line.
- Comparing two control trees becomes trivial. A simultaneous preorder traversal of two trees, comparing the corresponding nodes pair by pair, will determine a match.

In this chapter, we discuss how to convert the control trees into a canonical form and how to construct a tree of the i-vals by listing them in a canonical order. Let us first define some concepts.

DEFINITION 6.1: **Expression Tree:** A generalized expression tree is a rooted tree. Each internal node of the tree is labeled with an operator. Each leaf node is labeled with a numerical constant, a literal constant, an i-val identification, or a variable name. ∎

A control tree can be seen as a generalized expression tree, in which there are the conventional arithmetic operators ("add", "sub", "mul", etc.) and the operators we introduce ("control-group", "if-then-else", "array", "assignment", and others). Some operators are commutative. Changing the order of their children (their operands) does not change their semantics. Some operators are non-commutative.

We also recognize a third kind of operator that is **semi-commutative**. Changing the order of the children of such an operator may change the semantics due to other constraints. For a semi-commutative operator, only some of the orderings of its children can satisfy the constraints so as not to change the semantics. We call them the **valid orderings** of the children.

For the control tree, the operators are listed below according to their commutativity.

Commutative operators:
- "add", "mul", "max", "min",
- "eq", "ne", "and", "or", "eqv", "neqv"

Non-Commutative operators:

- "sub", "div", "exp", "mod",
- "ge", "gt", "le", "lt",
- "counter-loop", "pre-test-loop", "post-test-loop",
- "if-then", "if-then-else",
- "assignment", "array", "ival-group",
- "input", "output", "call"

Semi-commutative operators:

- "control-group"

Operators with one argument:

- "neg", "abs", "not",
- "return", "continue", "break",
- "pass-by-ref", "pass-by-val"

Changing the order of the statements listed under a "control-group" may change the semantics of the program, due to a data flow dependence that is not explicitly shown in the control tree. For the operator "control-group", the valid ordering of its children can be found through topological sorting of the data flow graph.

DEFINITION 6.2: **Isomorphic Expression Trees:** Two generalized expression trees are isomorphic if and only if the following conditions are true.

1. We can map one tree into the other by applying the following operations: Permute the children of the commutative operators. Preserve the order of children of the non-commutative operators. Permute the children of the semi-commutative operators to some valid orderings. In other words, after the permutations, the two trees should have the same shape.
2. The corresponding internal nodes represent the same operator.
3. The corresponding constant leaves represent the same constant.
4. There is a one-to-one renaming for the variables (respectively, i-val identifications) of one tree to the other tree, such that, after renaming, the variable names (respectively, i-val identifications) on the corresponding nodes are the same. ∎

The expression trees in Fig. 6.1 are isomorphic to each other. The expression trees in Fig. 6.2 are not isomorphic to each other.

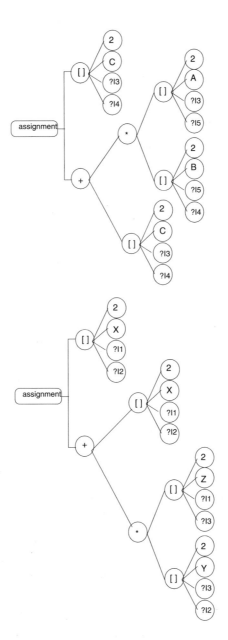

Figure 6.1
Isomorphic expression trees

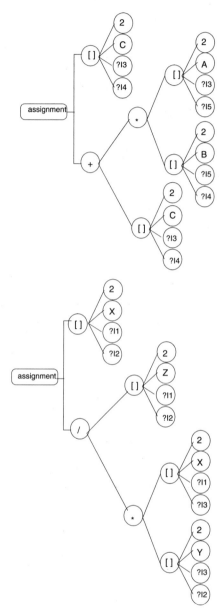

Figure 6.2
Non-isomorphic expression trees

THEOREM 6.1: Testing the isomorphism of two control trees, as generalized expression trees, is at least as difficult as graph isomorphism.

Proof. This proof resembles that of Thm. 2.1. The directed acyclic graph isomorphism problem can be reduced to control tree isomorphism as follows. Let G_1 and G_2 be two rooted directed acyclic graphs. Let P_1 and P_2 be their induced subprograms, respectively. Let T_1 and T_2 be the control trees of P_1 and P_2, respectively. It is easy to see that G_1 and G_2 are isomorphic if and only if T_1 and T_2 are isomorphic. ■

Checking whether a subprogram is an algorithmic instance of a pattern subprogram includes testing the isomorphism of their control trees. Due to its inherent difficulty, we shall not try to find a general deterministic algorithm to match the control tree of an extracted subprogram against a pattern control tree. Instead, we shall develop heuristic algorithms to turn the control trees into a canonical form. The control trees can then be compared node by node through a simultaneous preorder traversal of the trees. The heuristics should be strong enough to handle all cases that occur in practice. We work on the control tree representation instead of the general program dependence graph because heuristics for control tree isomorphism testing are more intuitive.

Our algorithm to convert a generalized expression tree into a canonical form consists of two steps.

1. Treating the semi-commutative operators as commutative operators, convert the expression tree into a canonical form using a technique called **expression tree orientation**. This results in an order for the children of each commutative and each semi-commutative operator. Details of this step are given in Sect. 6.2 and 6.3.

2. Based on the result of the previous step, reorder the children of each semi-commutative operator to comply with constraints. In the case of a control tree, this reordering can be done by a special version of topological sorting on the data flow dependence graph. The output sequence from a general topological sorting may not be unique, because there can be multiple candidate nodes ready to be output at one time. In our special version of topological sorting, the ordering obtained from the previous step can be used to determine uniquely which candidate to choose. Details are given in Sect. 6.4.

6.2 Orienting Expression Trees

DEFINITION 6.3: **Expression Tree Orientation:** Let $\models$ be a **linear order** on trees. Let T be a generalized expression tree. An **orientation** of T by $\models$ (denoted as $orientation(T)$ by $\models$) is a tree obtained by permuting the children of every commutative operator in such a way that the list of subtrees rooted at the children are sorted by $\models$. The lists of children for other operators remain unchanged. $\blacksquare$

It is easy to see that by computing the orientation of a generalized expression tree we can obtain a canonical ordering of the children of the commutative operators. Given an expression tree, assume that the nodes have been encoded with integers. The encoding has been performed such that two nodes are encoded the same if and only if they have the same label. We will discuss later how the encoding is done.

DEFINITION 6.4:   For generalized expression trees in which every node has an integer as its code, define three binary relations $\prec$ (read as less than), $\simeq$ (read as equal to) and $\preceq$ (less than or equal to) as follows. Let T_1 and T_2 be two trees.

1. $\preceq$ is simply $\prec$ or $\simeq$. That is,
$(T_1 \preceq T_2)$ *if and only if* $(T_1 \prec T_2) \parallel (T_1 \simeq T_2)$

2. For two single-node trees v_1 and v_2:
$v_1 \simeq v_2$ if and only if $code(v_1) = code(v_2)$.
$v_1 \prec v_2$ if and only if $code(v_1) < code(v_2)$.

3. Assume T_1 has root v_1 with subtrees $T_{1,1}$, $T_{1,2}$, ...$T_{1,k1}$ rooted at the children of v_1. Assume T_2 has root v_2 with subtrees $T_{2,1}$, $T_{2,2}$, ...$T_{2,k2}$ rooted at the children of v_2.
$T_1 \simeq T_2$ *if and only if* $k1 = k2$, $code(v_1) = code(v_2)$, and $T_{1,i} \simeq T_{2,i}$ ($i = 1, 2, ..., k1$).
$T_1 \prec T_2$ *if and only if* $(v_1, T_{1,1}, T_{1,2}, ..., T_{1,k1}) \prec (v_2, T_{2,1}, T_{2,2}, ..., T_{2,k2})$. Two tuples are compared in the same way two words are compared alphabetically in the dictionary. $\blacksquare$

It is obvious that $\preceq$ is a linear order. It is possible, therefore, to sort (by $\preceq$) trees whose nodes are encoded with integers.

DEFINITION 6.5:   **Rank:** Let α_1, α_2, ... α_n be a sequence of items sorted in non-decreasing order and let α be an item. We define the rank of α in the sequence to be the number of the items that are strictly less than α. Note that several items in the sequence can have the same rank. $\blacksquare$

Before we formally present the orientation algorithm based on $\preceq$, we shall describe the high level ideas. We assume that the nodes have been encoded with integers. The tree orientation permutes the order of children of each commutative operator, so that the list of subtrees rooted at the children of any commutative operator will be sorted according to linear order $\preceq$.

In other words, it constructs a new ordered list of children $C_v = (v_1, v_2, ..., v_k)$ for each node v representing a commutative operator, such that $subtree(v_1) \preceq subtree(v_2) \preceq ... \preceq subtree(v_k)$. In the algorithm, C_v will be computed in one big step for every commutative operator. The algorithm first computes L'_0, the sorted list of all the subtrees at level 0 and distributes them to the C_v lists of their parents. Consequently, all C_v lists at level 1 are then complete. In the next step, it computes L'_1, the sorted (by $\preceq$) list of the subtrees at level 1, and distribute them to the C_v lists of their parents. As a result, all the C_v lists at level 2 become complete. This continues until it reaches the root level.

Sorting the subtrees at level i (i.e., computing L'_i) requires only two things: the integer codes of their roots, and the ranks in L'_{i-1} of the subtrees at their children. It is unnecessary to look any levels lower than $i - 1$ to find out about the relative order of the subtrees.

After orientation, the children of each commutative operator are sorted according to $\preceq$. In this sorted list each of them has a rank which is called its **sibling rank**. For other operators, the sibling ranks of their children are just their positions from left to right among the siblings. Details of the algorithm are given in Fig. 6.3. First, we will define some notation.

DEFINITION 6.6:   **Tree Characteristics:** Let v be a node in a tree. The **depth** of v is the length of the path from the root to v. The **height** of v is the length of a longest path from v to a leaf in the subtree rooted at v. The **level** of v is the height of the tree minus the depth of v. ∎

With the correctness of the algorithm being obvious, we concentrate on the time complexity of the algorithm. Our algorithm needs a procedure to sort tuples of varying length. Fortunately, such a procedure is readily available. It is defined in Fig. 6.4.

LEMMA 6.1:   (String Sorting Lemma:) The procedure above sorts its input in time $O(l_{total} + m)$, where $l_{total} = \sum_{i=1}^{n} l_i$. Thm. 3.2 in (1)). ∎

A sequence of tuples can be sorted in time linear to the size of the range of their components plus the total number of components in all the tuples.

THEOREM 6.2:   Algorithm OrientTree runs in $O(|T|)$ time.

Proof. It is easy to see that the Initialization Steps (1-a) and (1-b) take $O(|T| + height(T)) = O(|T|)$ time. Step (1-c) can be done in $O(|T|)$ time by bucket sorting. Consider the Computation Steps. The Base Step requires $O(|L'_0|)$ time. In the Inductive

---

Procedure $OrientTree(T, T')$
Input: T: a tree, in which every node has been encoded with an integer in the range of $[0..|T|]$. (Two different nodes may have the same integer code.)
Output: T': $orientation(T)$ by $\preceq$. For a node v, C_v denote the list of children of v in the desired output order.
Variables:

1. L_i — the list of subtrees (in arbitrary order) at level i. ($i = 0, ..., height(T)$).
2. L_i' — the sorted (by $\preceq$ list of subtrees at level i. ($i = 0, 1, ..., height(T)$).
3. N_i — the list of all the nodes at level i sorted by their codes. ($i = 0, 1, ..., height(T)$).

Process:

/* Initialization Steps */
Traverse T (in preorder) and do the following:
Number the nodes in the order they are first visited.
Compute the level as well as the height for every node.
Link together all the subtrees at the same level. (The L_i denote the list of all subtrees at level i (for
        $i = 0, ..., height(T)$).)
for $i = 1$ **to** $height(T)$ **do**
$N_i \leftarrow NULL$;
Sort all the nodes (as individuals) of T by their codes.
Scan through this resulting sequence of nodes and do the following to each node v:
Let $i = level(v)$. Attach v to list N_i. Record the rank of v in N_i.
(The N_i are still sorted by their codes. Two different nodes in N_i can have the same rank if their codes are
        equal.)
/* Base Step */
Sort (by $\preceq$) the subtrees in L_0, resulting in list L_0'. (There is no need to do any sorting here. L_0' is the same as
the list N_0.)
Scan through L_0' again and do the following to each node v whose parent (if any) represents a commutative
operator:
Let w be the parent of v. Add v to the tail of list C_w. Record the rank of v in C_w.
/* Inductive steps */
for $i = 1$ **to** $height(T)$ **do**
Form a tuple for every subtree in L_i. Let v be the root of a subtree in L_i. Let $v_1, v_2, ..., v_k$ be the nodes in C_v.
Create a $(k + 1)$-tuple for v, $(a_0, a_1, a_2, ..., a_k)$ as follows: a_0 is the rank of v in N_i according to its code, a_1 is
        the rank of $subtree(v_1)$ in list L_{i-1}, a_2 is the rank of $subtree(v_2)$ in list L_{i-1}, and so on.
end
Sort the subtrees in L_i based on the tuples, resulting in sequence L_i'.
Scan through L_i' and do the following to each node v.
Let w (if any) be the parent of v. Add v to the tail of list C_w. Record the rank of v in C_w.

Figure 6.3
Algorithm to perform tree orientation

Procedure *LexSortStrings*
Input:

1. A sequence of string (tuples), $A_1, A_2, ..., A_n$, whose components are integers in the range 0 to $m - 1$. Let l_i be the length of $A_i = (a_{i1}, a_{i2}, ..., a_{il_i})$.

Output:

1. A permutation $B_1, B_2, ..., B_n$ of the A_i's such that $B_1 \leq B_2 \leq ... \leq B_n$.

Process:

 (see Algorithm 3.2 in (1)).

Figure 6.4
Algorithm to perform lexicographic sort of strings

Steps, the i-th iteration can be done $O(|L_i| + |L'_{i-1}|)$ time by Lemma 6.1. All iterations together take $O(\sum_{i=0}^{height(T)} |L_i|)$. Notice, by definition of L_i, we have $\sum_{i=0}^{height(T)} |L_i| = |T|$. Adding up for all the steps, the algorithm takes $O(|T|)$ time. ∎

6.3 An Expression Tree Encoding Scheme

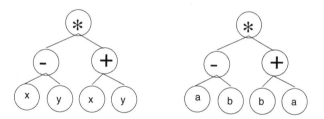

Figure 6.5
Two expression trees

Algorithm *OrientTree* assumes that the nodes of the input expression tree T are encoded with integers in the range $[0 \ldots |T|]$. Two nodes receive the same code if and only if they have the same node label. Encoding the nodes of T in this way is really a matter of encoding the distinct node labels on T.

The orientation is part of the process of turning the control trees into a canonical form. Two isomorphic control trees, as generalized expression trees, can be oriented to the same

```
(aab+bcc)(a+b+c)
(a-b)(b-c)(c-d)(d-a)(a+b+c+d)
(a+b+c+d)(a-b)(c-d)
(a+b+c+d)(a+b)(c+d)
(ab+bc+ca+de+ef+fg+ge)(a+b+c+d+e+f+g)
```

Figure 6.6
Difficult cases for distinguishing variables by context

shape so that corresponding nodes can be compared during pattern matching. Therefore, the encoding scheme should work consistently on different trees. Let T and T' be two isomorphic expression trees. Let x and x' be labels of the same category (variable, i-val identification, constant, operator) in T and T', respectively. The ideal encoding scheme should work in such a way that $code(x) = code(x')$ if and only if there is an isomorphism from T to T' that maps x to x'.

Finding the ideal encoding scheme is algorithmically at least as difficult as checking whether two control trees are isomorphic. A solution to the former can easily lead to a solution to latter. In the rest of the section, we give the details of our heuristic encoding algorithm.

Initial Encoding

The basic idea of the algorithm is to "sort" the labels of the generalized expression tree. Before the encoding begins, we collect all the distinct labels on the expression tree. We first sort the distinct labels by their categories (variable, i-val identification, constant, operator). Numerical constant labels are further sorted by their constant values. The relative ordering of all literal constants is predetermined since there is a fixed number of them. The same is true for operators.

Further sorting the variables and sorting the i-vals is non-trivial. It turns out that we can further sort them using the same method. In general, sorting variable names (respectively, i-vals) has to be done according to the ways the variable names (respectively, i-vals) are used in the whole expression tree. This is the most complex part and the only heuristic part of the encoding scheme. The encoding scheme needs to work consistently on different trees. Thus, when we sort the variables (respectively, i-vals), we must avoid using information such as the current ordering of the children of the commutative operators. In the case of variables, we must not sort them by their textual names from the source program.

We shall present the details of the encoding algorithm in two parts. The first part precisely encodes constants and operators. It also does initial encoding for variables and i-vals. This algorithm is presented in Fig. 6.7. The second part refines the codes for the variables (respectively, the i-vals). This algorithm is presented in Fig. 6.8.

Procedure *InitialEncoding*(T, DL, IC)
Input:

1. T: A generalized expression tree with n nodes.

Output:

1. DL: The list of distinct labels (each label remembers the nodes it is associated with).
2. IC: Integer codes in the range $[1 \ldots m]$ for all the labels on the input tree, where m is the number of distinct labels.

Process:

Collect all the distinct labels on the tree. Record the nodes with which each distinct label is associated.

Sort the labels by their categories, assuming the following order: *variable name, i-val, numerical constant, literal constant, operator.*

Process each category of labels according to the following cases.

case 1: Further sort variables by tuples assigned to them as follows.

For each variable V, assign to V a tuple consisting of the following:

the dimension of the variable (0 for scalar),

the number of occurrences, of V on the tree,

the depths in the expression tree, of the occurrences listed in non-decreasing order,

the integer code of the variable's base data type, (*integer*, *logical*, etc.).

case 2: Further sort I-vals by tuples assigned to them as follows.

For each i-val I, assign to I a tuple consisting of the following:

the nesting level of the loop to which I belongs,

the number of occurrences of I in the tree,

the depths in the expression tree of the occurrences listed in non-decreasing order.

case 3: Further sort numerical constants by their values.

case 4: Further sort literal constants by a predefined ordering.

Generate the predefined ordering by storing all possible literal constants in a vector. This can be done because there is a fixed number of them.

case 5: Further sort operators by a predefined ordering.

Generate this ordering by storing all the possible operators in a vector. This can be done because there is a fixed number of them.

Let L_1, L_2, ..., L_m ($m \leq n$) be the sorted sequence of distinct labels from the previous steps. For each L_i ($1 \leq i \leq m$), set $code(L_i)$ to be its rank in the sequence.

Figure 6.7
Algorithm to perform initial encoding

The following theorem is obvious.

THEOREM 6.3:   Given as input an n-node expression tree, Algorithm $Initial Encoding$ runs in $O(n \log n)$ time in the worst case.

Proof. Except for Case 3, all other steps take $O(n)$ time by radix sort (1). Case 3 takes $O(n \log n)$ time. ∎

In practice, the number of numerical constants occurring in a program is extremely small compared to the size of the program. Therefore, the following corollary is also obvious.

COROLLARY 6.1:   Given as input an n-node expression tree, Algorithm $Initial Encoding$ runs in $O(n)$ expected time. ∎

Refining the Codes

Before we present a heuristic algorithm to refine the codes for both variables and i-vals, we will see why refining the codes is necessary. Encoding is part of the process that converts the expression tree into a canonical form. This makes it possible to turn two isomorphic expression trees into the same shape. The variables in the corresponding nodes can then be matched consistently through a one-to-one renaming.

Consider an example in Fig. 6.5. These two expression trees are isomorphic. If we try to match the corresponding nodes by the current shapes of the trees, we will not be able to obtain a consistent match for the variables. Using only the codes produced by Algorithm $Initial Encoding$, in which $code(x) = code(y) = 1$, $code(-) = 2$, $code(+) = 3$, and $code(*) = 4$ for the first tree, and for the second tree $code(a) = code(b) = 1$, $code(-) = 2$, $code(+) = 3$, and $code(*) = 4$, Algorithm $Orient Tree$ will not reorder the children of operator "+". Therefore, in order to obtain a canonical form for the trees, we must refine the codes for the variables.

Our strategy is to **distinguish and sort** variables according to the ways they are used in the generalized expression tree. For convenience, we only mention variables when we explain the ideas of the algorithm.

Sometimes, some variables are indistinguishable, regardless of their textual names, from the context of the generalized expression tree. For example, in expression $aab + bcc$ variables a and b can be distinguished by their usage in the expression. In contrast, the ways that variables a and c are used in the expression are not distinguishable. Any ordering between a and c will serve our purpose because of the rules for variable renaming during pattern matching. The ways variables a, b, c, d are used in expression $(a - b)(b - c)(c - d)(d - a)(a + b + c + d)$ are also indistinguishable. It is easy to see that there is some kind of "cycle", $a \rightarrow b \rightarrow c \rightarrow d \rightarrow a$. Any ordering of the variables along this "cycle" (for example, c, d, a, b) will be fine for our purpose of pattern matching.

DEFINITION 6.7: **Symmetric Expressions:** Two expressions are symmetric if one can be obtained from the other by permuting the operands of the commutative operators.

Let $E(x_1, x_2, ..., x_k, ...)$ be an expression. We say that variables x_1, x_2, ..., x_k form a **symmetric cycle** if and only if expressions $E(x_1, x_2, ..., x_k, ...)$ and $E(y_1, y_2, ..., y_k, ...)$ are symmetric, where sequence $y_1, y_2, ..., y_k$ is from ANY cyclic shifting of sequence x_1, $x_2, ..., x_k$. ∎

There are other situations in which we say that the variables are in an indirectly symmetric cycle. For example, in expression $(a-b)(c-d)(e-f)(a+b+c+d+e+f)$ variables a, c, and e can be distinguished only if we can distinguish variables b, d, and f, and vice versa.

DEFINITION 6.8: **Indirectly Symmetric Cycle:**

Let $E(a_{1,1}, ..., a_{1,p}, a_{2,1}, ..., a_{2,p}, ..., a_{k,1}, ..., a_{k,p}, ...)$ be an expression. If the following expressions are pairwise symmetric,

- $E(a_{1,1}, ..., a_{1,p}, a_{2,1}, ..., a_{2,p}, ..., a_{k,1}, ..., a_{k,p}, ...)$
- $E(a_{1,p}, a_{1,1}..., a_{1,p-1}, a_{2,p}, a_{2,1}..., a_{2,p-1}, a_{k,p}, a_{k,1}..., a_{k,p-1})$
- $E(a_{1,p-1}, a_{1,p}..., a_{1,p-2}, a_{2,p-1}, a_{2,p}..., a_{2,p-2}, a_{k,p-1}, a_{k,p}..., a_{k,p-2})$
- ...
- $E(a_{1,2}, ..., a_{1,p}, a_{1,1}, a_{2,2}, ..., a_{2,p}, a_{2,1}a_{k,2}, ..., a_{k,p}, a_{k,1})$

we say that each of the following variable groups forms an indirectly symmetric cycle.

- $a_{1,1}, a_{1,2}, ..., a_{1,p}$
- $a_{2,1}, a_{2,2}, ..., a_{2,p}$
- ...
- $a_{k,1}, a_{k,2}, ..., a_{k,p}$

These indirectly symmetric cycles are said to be related. ∎

We can have two similar definitions for the i-vals.

The algorithm uses a list of heuristics, based on invariants of the variables in the expression tree, to distinguish the variables. If a group of variables cannot be distinguished by the invariants, we will randomly make a variable "smaller" than the rest of variables in the group. The process of distinguishing the rest of the variables in the group then continues.

Our inability to distinguish a group of variables does not mean they form a symmetric cycle. It also does not mean that they are in an indirectly symmetric cycle. The invariants to distinguish the variables are based on two basic properties: symmetricness and indirect symmetricness. There could be other basic properties. In the case that the variables are really in a symmetric cycle, it will be sufficient to "break the cycle" by making one variable "smaller" than the rest of the group. In the case that the variables are in an indirectly symmetric cycle, this will help break that cycle and other related cycles.

Our heuristics resemble the numerous heuristic algorithms proposed to encode general graphs for isomorphism testing. (See (45) for a survey.) It is tempting to suppose that from these invariants we can develop some theoretically complete invariants. It does not appear to be possible, just as in the case of graph isomorphism testing (45). We seek heuristics that are sufficient to distinguish variables in practical application domains. We intend to make them strong enough (i.e. sufficient) for that purpose. Our algorithm is designed in such a way that we can always add more invariants as we learn from the cases that, in practice, the existing heuristics fail to distinguish.

We provide the list of examples in Fig. 6.6 for understanding the algorithm. To get a feel about the strength of the heuristics, note that three out of four of them will be enough to distinguish the variables in all these examples. But we still present all of the heuristics to handle more situations that may occur in practice.

Read and Corneil (45) conclude their paper on graph isomorphism with the following remarks.

"many algorithm-builders attempt to gain some idea of how good their isomorphism algorithm is by running it on a large number of graphs, often constructed at random. This is likely to be quite misleading, since most graphs present no great problem even to badly designed algorithms. The test of a graph isomorphism algorithm is how it behaves under 'worst case' conditions, i.e., how it handles the really recalcitrant graphs such as those just described."

Analogous comments are just as true of mapping variables from an extracted subprogram to a pattern. Most of the time, the problem is very straightforward. The true test of our heuristics only comes with the pathological cases.

Now we give the algorithms of each of the procedures called in the RefineCode algorithm. These are found in Fig(s). 6.9, 6.12, 6.15, and 6.18.

These procedures use invariants of the variables (or i-vals) to split a group of variables (or i-vals) currently sharing the same code.

The procedure defined in Fig. 6.9 splits a group of variables (or i-vals) G by comparing an invariant called the instance-tree. The idea here is that two variables (or two i-vals) are distinguishable only when their instance-trees cannot be turned into the same tree

---

Procedure $RefineCode(T, IC, code)$
Input:

1. T: A generalized expression tree with n nodes,

2. IC: The sequence of distinct labels output by procedure $InitialEncoding$. For convenience in the presentation, we will assume that the list of distinct labels output by $InitialEncoding$ is $C_1, ..., C_p, O_1, ..., O_q, V_1, ..., V_s, I_1, ..., I_t$ where the C's are the distinct constants (numerical or literal), the O's are the distinct operators, the V's are the distinct variables, and the I's are the distinct i-vals.

3. $code(V_i)$ ($i = 1, ..., s$): the current code in the range $[(p + q) + 1, (p + q) + s]$. (Different variables may now be sharing the same code.)

Output:

1. $code(V_k)$ (for $k = 1, ..., s$): in the range $[(p + q) + 1, (p + q) + s]$ such that $code(V_i) \neq code(V_j)$ if $i \neq j$.
2. $code(I_k)$ (for $k = 1, ..., t$): in the range $[(p + q + s) + 1, (p + q + s) + t]$ such that $code(I_i) \neq code(I_j)$ if $i \neq j$.

Process:

/* (Step A) Distinguish variables by their invariants */

Group $V_1, V_2, ..., V_s, I_1, ..., I_t$. by their current codes. Let GL be the list of all the groups with multiple members. (Variables and i-vals will never be in the same group.)

for (each group G in GL) **do**

call $SplitGroupByInstanceTrees(T, G)$;

for (each group G in GL) **do**

call $SplitGroupByDistanceGraph(T, G, GL, code)$;

repeat

for (each group G in GL) **do**

    call $SplitGroupByPathsToRoot(T, G)$;

until (GL is unchanged)

/* (Step B) Break the groups with a little randomness */

repeat

if (GL is not empty) **then**

    Let G be the first group. Pick any member e from G and split it from G by making it "smaller" than the rest of group.

    call $UpdateCodesGroup(code, \{e\}, G - \{e\})$ (Update the codes to reflect this split.)

    Put group $G - \{e\}$ back into GL.

endif

repeat

    for (each group G in GL) **do**

        call $SplitGroupByPathsToRoot(T, G)$;

until (GL is unchanged)

until (GL is empty)

Figure 6.8
Algorithm to refine encoding

by orientation. In other words, the orientations of their instance-trees being identical is a necessary condition for the variables to be indistinguishable.

Procedure $SplitGroupByInstanceTrees(T, G, GL, code)$
Input:

1. T: the expression tree,
2. G: a group of variables (or i-vals) to be split,
3. GL: the list of the groups to be split,
4. $code$: an array of records recording the labels and their current integer codes. For presentation, we use $code(L)$ to denote the code for L.

Output:

1. $GL, code$ (These two structures will be updated after splitting G.)

Process:

> **for** (each member v in G) **do**
>> Associate with v an instance-tree constructed from expression tree T: The instance-tree has exactly the same shape as T. The corresponding internal nodes represent operators with the same commutativity (either commutative or non-commutative). Each node of the instance-tree is given an integer code which is the current code of the corresponding node on T.
>> **for** (every node N in instance-tree) **do**
>>> **if** (the code of $N \geq code(v)$) **then**
>>>> Increment the code of N by 1;
>>> **endif**
>> **end**
>> For the nodes in the instance-tree corresponding to label v, reset their integer codes to $code(v)$, which is the current code of v on T.
> **end**
> Sort the orientations of the instance-trees $T_1, ..., T_g$, where $g = |G|$. This can be done by computing the orientation of a tree rooted with a null node, containing all the instance trees as branches, using procedure $OrientTree$.
> Based on the result of sorting, partition G into subgroups $G_1, G_2, ..., G_k$.
> **call** $UpdateCodesGroup(code, G_1, G_2, ..., G_k)$
> Add the multi-member subgroups in $G_1, G_2, ..., G_k$ back into GL. (Assuming G has been removed from GL)

Figure 6.9
Algorithm to split groups by instance trees

LEMMA 6.2: The time complexity of Procedure $SplitGroupByInstanceTrees$ is $O(|G| \times |T|)$ time.

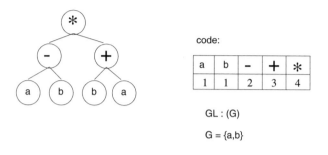

code:

a	b	-	+	*
1	1	2	3	4

GL : (G)

G = {a,b}

Input to Procedure

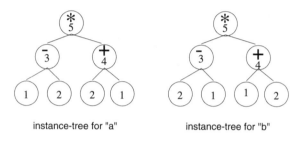

instance-tree for "a"   instance-tree for "b"

After step (1)

Figure 6.10
Steps of procedure $SplitGroupByInstanceTrees$, part 1

Proof. Step 1 takes $O(|G| \times |T|)$ time. Step 2 takes $O(|G| \times |T|)$ time according to Thm. 6.2. Step 3 takes $O(|G|)$ time because it makes one pass through the sequence. Step 4 takes $O(|T|)$ time. Step 5 needs $O(|G|)$ time because it makes one pass through all the groups. ■

The procedure defined in Fig. 6.12 splits a group of variables (or i-vals) G by decomposing the **c-distance graph** The c-distance graph is a perfect undirected graph with its vertices being the members of G. Each arc of the graph has a weight that represents the **c-distance** (collective distance) between its two end points. Let v_1 and v_2 be two members in G, each member having r occurrences in the input expression tree being encoded. The c-distance between v_1 and v_2 is defined to be a sorted tuple of r^2 integers that are the distances in T from every occurrence of v_1 to every occurrence of v_2. The idea here is that v_1 and v_2 are distinguishable if there is a v_3 in G such that $c - distance(v_1, v_3) \neq c - distance(v_2, v_3)$. .

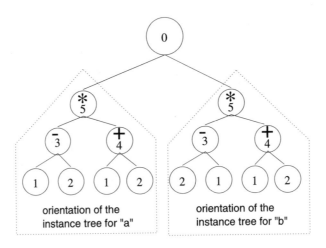

After step (2)

G1 = {a}   G2 = {b}

After step (3)

a	b	–	+	*
1	2	3	4	5

After step (4)

GL = ()

After step (5)

Figure 6.11
Steps of procedure *SplitGroupByInstanceTrees*, part 2

LEMMA 6.3:   The time complexity of Procedure *SplitGroupByDistanceGraph* is bounded by $O(r^2 \times |G|^2 + |T|)$, where r is the number of occurrence of a member of G in the expression tree T.

Proof. Before Step 1, preprocess T in $O(|T|)$ time using the algorithms in (23) and (51) so that, after preprocessing, the lowest common ancestor between any pair of nodes on T can be found in $O(1)$. At the same time, precompute the depth of each node in T. After these preprocessing steps, the distance between every pair of nodes can be determined in $O(1)$, by adding up their distances to their lowest common ancestor. Step 1 needs to

---

Procedure $SplitGroupByDistanceGraph(T, G, GL, code)$
Input:

1. T: the expression tree,
2. G: a group of variables (or i-vals) to be split,
3. GL: the list of the groups to be split,
4. $code$: an array of records recording the labels and their current integer codes. For presentation, we use $code(L)$ to denote the code for L.

Output:

1. $GL, code$ (These two structures will be updated after splitting G.)

Process:

Compute the c-distance between every pair of members in G.

Select the distinct c-distances, and sort them. In the succeeding steps, each c-distance will be represented by an integer which is its rank in this sorted list. (Two c-distances may have the same rank if they are equal.)

Build a perfect graph with the members of G as its vertices. Assign to each arc an integer rank identifying the c-distance between the two ends.

Partition group G into subgroups such that, for any v_1 and v_2 in G, v_1 and v_2 belong to the same subgroup if and only if for every v_3 in G, we have $c - distance(v_1, v_3) \neq c - distance(v_2, v_3)$. (With the same subgroup, the c-distance between any pair of variables is always the same value.)

Sort the subgroups using the following numbers associated with each subgroup: **cardinality** (1) of the subgroup, and (2) the c-distance between any two members in the subgroup. Assume a c-distance of zero if the subgroup has only one member.

In the sorted list of subgroups, merge the ones that have the same rank. Two subgroups are merged if they have the cardinality and c-distance between their own members. (We merge these subgroups back because at this point we are not able to decide which subgroup should be given a relatively smaller integer code.) Let the resultant list (still sorted) of subgroups be $G_1, G_2, ..., G_k$.

call $UpdateCodesBySplittingGroup(G_1, G_2, ..., G_k)$

Add the multi-member subgroups in $G_1, G_2, ..., G_k$ back into GL. (Assuming G has been removed from GL)

Figure 6.12
Algorithm to split groups by distance graphs

compute r^2 distances for each of the $|G|^2$ pairs of members in G. So Step 1 requires $O(r^2 \times |G|^2 + |T|)$ time. Step 2 can be done in $O(|G|^2 \times r^2)$ times by Lemma 6.1 (the String Sorting Lemma). Step 3 requires $O(|G|^2)$ time. Step 4 can be done in $O(|G|^2)$ time, using the algorithm in (35). Step 5 can be done in $O(|G|)$ time by bucket sorting. Step 6. can be done in $O(|G|)$ time. Step 7 takes no more than $O(|G| + |T|)$ time. Step 8 takes $O(|G|)$ time. Adding them up for all steps, the time complexity of the algorithm is $O(r^2 \times |G|^2 + |T|)$. ∎

The procedure defined in Fig. 6.15 splits a group of variables (or i-vals) G by comparing the integer labeled paths from the variable occurrence to the root of the tree.

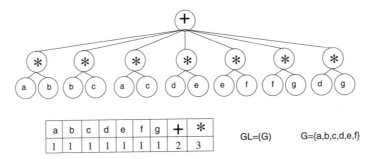

	a	b	c	d	e	f	g
a		(2,4,4,4)	(2,4,4,4)	(4,4,4,4)	(4,4,4,4)	(4,4,4,4)	(4,4,4,4)
b			(2,4,4,4)	(4,4,4,4)	(4,4,4,4)	(4,4,4,4)	(4,4,4,4)
c				(4,4,4,4)	(4,4,4,4)	(4,4,4,4)	(4,4,4,4)
d					(2,4,4,4)	(2,4,4,4)	(2,4,4,4)
e						(2,4,4,4)	(2,4,4,4)
f							(2,4,4,4)

After step (1)

(2,4,4,4) (4,4,4,4)

After step (2)

Figure 6.13
Steps of procedure $SplitGroupByDistanceGraph$, part 1

LEMMA 6.4: The time complexity of Procedure $SplitGroupByPathsToRoot$ is bounded by $O(r \times |G| \times |T|)$, where r is the number of occurrence of a member of G in the expression tree T.

Proof. Step 1 takes $O(|T|)$ time. Steps 2-4 require $O(r \times |G| \times |T|)$ in the worst case. Steps 5-6 can be done in $O(|T|)$ time. ∎
The following lemma is obvious.

LEMMA 6.5: Procedure $UpdateCodesAfterSplittingGroup$ can be implemented in $O(m)$ time, where m is the total number of distinct labels in the input expression tree. ∎

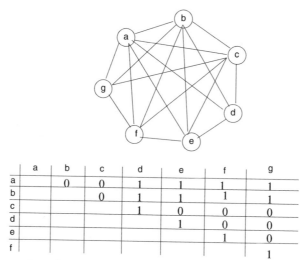

	a	b	c	d	e	f	g
a		0	0	1	1	1	1
b			0	1	1	1	1
c				1	0	0	0
d					1	0	0
e						1	0
f							1

the c-distance graph and its matrix representation

After step (3)

G1={a,b,c}   G2={d,e,f,g}

After steps (4)-(5)

a	b	c	d	e	f	g	+	*
1	1	1	2	2	2	2	3	4

After step (7)

GL = (G1,G2)

After step (8)

Figure 6.14
Steps of procedure *SplitGroupByDistanceGraph*, part 2

THEOREM 6.4:   Algorithm *RefineCode* takes $O(|T|^2 \times (s + t))$ time, where T is the expression tree to be encoded. s is the number of distinct variables in T. t is the number of distinct i-val references in T.

Proof. Consider first Step A. (A.1) takes $O(s + t)$ by integer bucket sorting. (A.2)

Procedure $SplitGroupByPathsToRoot(T, G, GL, code)$
Input:

1. T: the expression tree,
2. G: a group of variables (or i-vals) to be split,
3. GL: the list of the groups to be split,
4. *code*: an array of records recording the labels and their current integer codes. For presentation, we use $code(L)$ to denote the code for L.

Output:

1. GL, *code* (These two structures will be updated after splitting G.)

Process:

Compute orientation of the expression tree based on the current encoding.

for (every v in G) **do**

Assume v has r occurrences in T. For each occurrence of v, make a tuple $t(v)$ of integers representing the sibling ranks of the nodes on the path from this occurrence to the root of T.

Sort the tuples thus created for the occurrences of v. Let $t_1(v), t_2(v), ..., t_r(v)$ be the sorted sequence of tuples.

Form a tuple of r tuples $(t_1(v), ..., t_r(v))$ and associate it with v.

end

Sort the members of G by their tuples (of tuples) formed in the previous step. Group the members with equal tuples (of tuples). This is to partition G into subgroups $G_1, G_2, ..., G_k$.

call $UpdateCodesBySplittingGroup(G_1, G_2, ..., G_k, code)$

Add the multi-member subgroups in $G_1, G_2, ..., G_k$ back into GL, Assuming G has been removed from GL.

Figure 6.15
Algorithm to split groups by paths to root

involves calling algorithm $SplitGroupByInstanceTrees()$. Each call takes $O(|T| \times |G|)$ time. All iterations together, (A.2) takes no more than $O(|T| \times (s+t))$, because the total size of all such G is bounded by $(s + t)$. (A.3) calls $SplitGroupByDistanceGraph()$. Each call takes no more than $O(|T|^2)$ time. All iterations in the loop nest together (A.3) can be done in $O(|T|^2 \times (s+t))$, because there are no more than $(s+t)$ groups to be split. Similar to the analysis for (A.3), the time complexity of (A.4) is also bounded by $O(|T|^2 \times (s+t))$. So the time complexity of Step A is bounded by $O(|T|^2 \times (s + t))$. Also similar to the analysis for (A.3), the time complexity of Step B is bounded by $O(|T|^2 \times (s+t))$. ∎

6.4 Adjusting Children of control-group Nodes

The tree orientation has arranged the children of each control-group node into a canonical order. This **oriented order** of the statements under the same control-group, however, may

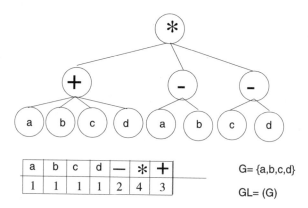

Input to procedure

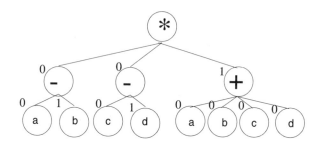

**After step (1), the integer
by each node is its sibling rank**

Figure 6.16
Steps of procedure *SplitGroupByPathsToRoot*, part 1

violate the semantics of the program due to data flow dependencies. Here, we show how to adjust this canonical order to comply with the data flow dependence. The adjustment is done in such a way that the resultant ordering will be uniquely determined, in other words, it also will be canonical.

Statement Ordering and Data Flow Dependences

Consider two children statements S_1 and S_2 of a control-group node. If there is a data flow dependence, either directly or indirectly, from S_1 to S_2 but none from S_2 to S_1, any ordering in which S_1 occurs before S_2 will satisfy this particular data flow dependence relationship.

Tuples formed for the variables

a: ((0,0),(1,0))

b: ((0,1),(1,0))

c: ((0,0),(1,0))

d: ((0,1),(1,0))

After step (2)

G1= {a,c}   G2= {b,d}

After step (3)

a	b	c	d	—	*	+	
1	2	1	2	3	5	4	

After step (4)

GL = (G1, G2)

After step (5)

Figure 6.17
Steps of procedure $SplitGroupByPathsToRoot$, part 2

If there is no data flow dependence between S_1 and S_2, the relative order of S_1 and S_2 will not be important. If there is a data flow dependence from S_1 to S_2 and one from S_2 to S_1, then the relative order of S_1 and S_2 from source program must be maintained. A valid ordering of a control-group's children can be computed from the statement-level data flow dependence graph G (Sect. 5.6) for the children statements of the control-group node.

If such a graph G is acyclic, any topological sorting is a valid one. If G is cyclic, a topological sort cannot be done on G directly. We introduce the concept of vertex collapsing.

DEFINITION 6.9:   **Vertex Collapsing:** Let G be a graph. Let V_1, V_2, ..., V_k be disjoint subsets of the vertices in G. Simultaneous vertex collapsing of V_1, V_2, ..., V_k in G means the construction of a new graph G' as follows.

(i)   Each vertex in G' represents a group of the vertices of G, which is either equal to one of V_i ($i = 1, ..., k$) or composed of just a single vertex not in any of V_i ($i = 1, ..., k$). (For convenience, we say that the group of vertices of G is collapsed into a single vertex of G')

Procedure $UpdateCodesAfterSplittingGroup(code, G_1, ..., G_k)$
Input:

1. *code*
2. $G_1, ..., G_k$: the list of subgroups from splitting a larger group.

Output:

1. *code*: an array of records recording the labels and their current integer codes. For presentation, we use $code(L)$ to denote the code for L.

Process:

   for $i = 1, k$
   for (each member v in G_i) **do**
          Assign a two-element tuple (c, i) to v, where c is v's current code.
   for (each label v not in any of $G_1, ..., G_k$) **do**
   Assign to v a one-element tuple which is its current code.
   Sort all the labels by the tuples thus assigned. Record the new code of every label as its new rank.

Figure 6.18
Algorithm to update codes after splitting groups

(ii)   There is a (directed) arc between u_1 and u_2 of G' if and only if there is a (directed) arc between the groups they represent.

When collapsing vertices of a data flow dependence graph, we ignore the arc types (output-dependence, anti-dependence, and true-dependence). ∎

For example, consider a directed graph G. It is easy to see that collapsing a **strongly connected component** into a single node u will not introduce a new cycle containing u in the resultant graph. Collapsing all the strongly connected components in G will result in a directed acyclic graph.

Let G be the statement-level data flow dependence graph on the children statements of a control-group node v. Let G' be the resultant graph obtained by collapsing all strongly connected components in G. A valid ordering of these children statements can be computed as follows. Compute a topologically sorted sequence of the vertices of G'. Replace in the topological sequence each such vertex of G' representing a strongly connected component G with component's vertices, listed in the same order as in the source program.

An Algorithm to Adjust the control-group Children

Our purpose is to obtain a canonical and valid ordering of the children statements of a control-group node. Tree orientation has given us the canonical order, e.g. the oriented order. A special topological sort on the collapsed statement-level data flow dependence graph gives a valid ordering. There can be many different such valid orderings, however, because there can be many topological orders. To get a unique topological order, we can use the oriented order to select a candidate from those whose predecessors in the collapsed graph have been chosen.

In summary, we need two pieces of information to compute a special **topological sorting** on G:

- Use the oriented order of the children to select among the eligible components (groups).

- Use the source code order to list the nodes in each component.

The details of the algorithm are given in Fig. 6.19 and 6.20. The new ordering will incorporate as much as possible the ordering obtained from orientation and yet without violating the data flow dependence.

THEOREM 6.5:   The time complexity of Algorithm $AdjustControlGroup(T)$ takes $O(|T| + \sum_{i=1}^{m}(|E_i| + |V_i| \times \log|V_i|))$ time, where $G_i = (V_i, E_i)$ $(i = 1, ..., m)$ are the the statement-level data flow dependence graphs on control tree T.

Proof. For each statement-level data flow dependence graph $G_i = (V_i, E_i)$, Steps 1 and 2 take $O(|E_i| + |V_i|)$ time. In Step 3, the Initialization steps take $O(|V_i|)$ time. The while-loops altogether take $O(|E_i| + |V_i| \times \log|V_i|)$ time, where the $|V_i| \times \log|V_i|$ factor is due to the priority queue operations for the $candidateList$.

The total time complexity of the algorithm depends on the number and sizes of the statement-level data flow dependence graphs associated with the control-group nodes. Traversing T takes $O(|T|)$ time. Assume $G_i = (V_i, E_i)$ $(i = 1, ..., m)$ are all the statement-level data flow dependence graphs on T. Adding up for the whole control tree, the call to $specialTopologicalSort()$ requires $O(\sum_{i=1}^{m}(|E_i| + |V_i| \times \log|V_i|))$ time. ∎

To get a feel of the time complexity, note that $|V_i|$ is the number of children of a control-group node, and it is usually small. All $|V_i|$ together are still smaller than $|T|$. In any case, $|E_i| \le |V_i|^2$. So the time complexity is loosely bounded from above by $O(|T|^2)$.

Procedure $AdjustControlGroup(T, G)$
Input:

1. T: The control tree after orientation.
2. $G(CN)$ For each control-group node CN in T, a statement-level data flow dependence graph $G(CN)$ on the children of CN. (Refer to Sect. 5.6.) Each node v of $G(CN)$ is associated with two integers $sourcePosition(v)$, and $orientedPosition(v)$, respectively representing v's positions among its siblings before and after the tree orientation of T.

Output:

1. T: with the children of every control-group node adjusted to comply with the data flow dependencies.

Variables:

1. L: This is used to keep the output during a special topological ordering of the vertices of $G(CN)$.

Process:

  for (each control-group node CN in T) **do**

  Let $G(CN)$ be the statement-level data flow dependence graph for the children statements of CN. Find all the strongly connected components in $G(CN)$ $s_1, s_2, ..., s_q$, using Tarjan's algorithm (48).

  In graph $G(CN)$, collapse s_i ($1 \le i \le q$) into a special node α_i. Let G' be the resultant acyclic graph. Assign to α_i ($1 \le i \le q$) an integer $weight(\alpha_i) = \min_{v \in s_i}(orientedPosition(v))$.

  Assign to other nodes u of G' an integer $weight(u)$ equal to $orientedPosition(u)$.

  /* Perform a prioritized topological sorting on G' */

  $L = NULL$

  call $PriorityTopSort(G', L)$

  In sequence L, substitute each α_i ($1 \le i \le q$) with the vertices of s_i, listed nondecreasingly according to integers by $sourcePosition()$. Let $v_1, v_2, ..., v_m$ be the resultant sequence.

  Reorder the children of CN as $v_1, v_2, ..., v_m$.

  end

Figure 6.19
Algorithm to adjust control groups

6.5 Representing Induction Values

After turning the control tree into a canonical form, we can list the i-vals of the program in a canonical order.

Listing the Induction Values in a Canonical Order

First, we need to list the i-vals in a canonical order. We only list the i-vals as they appear under the **ival-group** node in the control tree. We do not list those references of i-vals in

---

Procedure *PriorityTopSort*(G', L)
Input:

1. G' Acyclic statement-level data flow dependence graph.

Output:

1. L: This is used to keep the output during a special topological ordering of the vertices of $G(CN)$.

Variables:

1. *candidateList*: This is a list of nodes whose predecessors have been output during topological sorting.
2. *predCount*(v): This is used to keep track of the number of predecessors of v that have not been output during topological sorting.

Process:

  candidateList = *NULL*;
  for (each node w in G') **do**
  predCount(w) =the number of predecessors of w in G';
  for (each node v in G') **do**
  if (*predCount*(v) = 0) **then**
      Add v to *candidateList*;
  end
  while (*candidateList* $\neq$ *NULL*) **do**
  Remove from *candidateList* a node u with the smallest *weight*(u);
  Output u to L;
  for (each successor w of u) **do**
      predCount(w) = *predCount*(w) − 1;
      if (*predCount*(w) = 0) **then**
         Add w to *candidateList*;
  end
  end

Figure 6.20
Algorithm to perform prioritized topological sort

the simple statements. All we need do is to perform a preorder traversal of the control tree and list the i-vals under the ival-group nodes in the order they are visited. Let the i-vals thus listed be:

$$?I_1, ?I_2, ..., ?I_k$$

Hereafter, besides the compiler-generated identification, we also will use integer j ($1 \leq j \leq k$) as the identification of i-val I_j, especially when we need to compare i-val references in two control trees during pattern matching.

Setting Up the I-val Tree

For the purpose of matching the i-vals of two subprograms (to be discussed in Sect. 7.2), it is convenient to have a tree of induction values, the **i-val tree**. Assume the i-vals of the subprogram are listed in a canonical order as the following:

$?I_1$: $(B_1(x_1, x_2, ..., x_n), E_1(x_1, x_2, ..., x_n),$
$S_1(x_1, x_2, ..., x_n))$
$?I_2$: $(B_2(x_1, x_2, ..., x_n, ?I_1), E_2(x_1, x_2, ..., x_n, ?I_1),$
$S_2(x_1, x_2, ..., x_n, ?I_1))$
$?I_3$: $(B_3(x_1, x_2, ..., x_n, ?I_1, ?I_2), E_3(x_1, x_2, ..., x_n, ?I_1, ?I_2),$
$S_3(x_1, x_2, ..., x_n, ?I_1, ?I_2))$

......

$?I_k$: $(B_k(x_1, x_2, ..., x_n, ?I_1, ..., ?I_{k-1}), E_k(x_1, x_2, ..., x_n, ?I_1, ..., ?I_{k-1}),$
$S_k(x_1, x_2, ..., x_n ?I_1, ..., ?I_{k-1}))$

The x_j ($j = 1, ..., n$) are free variables. $?I_i$ ($i = 1, ..., k$) are (compiler generated) identifications for the ivals. $B_i(x_1, ..., x_n, ?I_1, ..., ?I_{i-1})$,
$E_i(x_1, ..., x_n, ?I_1, ..., ?I_{i-1})$, and $S_i(x_1, ..., x_n, ?I_1, ..., ?I_{i-1})$ ($i = 1, .., k$) are expressions of free variables $x_1, x_2, ..., x_n$ and i-vals. $?I_1, ..., ?I_{i-1}$ are converted into a format as specified by the grammar in Fig. 5.17.

The i-val tree of the subprogram is shown in Fig. 6.21, where the triangles containing $T(B_1), T(E_1), T(S_1), ..., T(S_k)$ stand for the parse trees of expressions $B_1, E_1, S_1, ..., S_k$ according to the grammar in Fig. 5.17. It is easy to see that the i-val tree can be set up in linear time.

6.6 Remarks

In the representation of the i-val, if there is a $\max(E_1, E_2)$ or $\min(E_1, E_2)$ function, we will not be able to list the parameters (E_1, E_2) in a canonical order. E_1 and E_2 may contain free variables that can later be substituted by expressions. Thus, no linear order on such parameters can be defined.

In practice, the parameters of functions $\max(E_1, E_2)$ or $\min(E_1, E_2)$ used in i-vals tend to be simple. One of them is very often a constant. Such situations can be easily

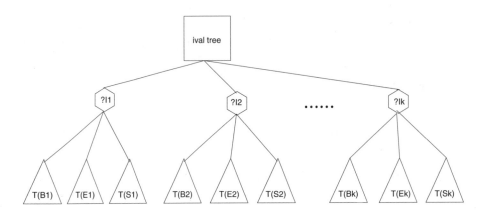

Figure 6.21
An i-val tree

handled by simple heuristics. For example, we can list the constant before the non-constant expressions.

6.7 Summary

• To compare an extracted subprogram with a pattern efficiently, we convert the control tree into a canonical form, and list the i-vals in a canonical order.

• Tree orientation reorders the children of commutative and semi-commutative operators based on an encoding of the nodes of the control tree.

• Encoding the nodes of a control tree involves encoding the node labels of that tree.

• Variable and i-val nodes are encoded with respect to their context in the whole control tree representing the subprogram.

• Our algorithm uses a series of heuristics, based on the invariants of the variables (and the i-vals) in the control tree, to distinguish the variables.

• Our heuristics resemble those used to encode graphs for isomorphism testing.

• The oriented order of the children statements of a control-group node must be adjusted according to the data flow dependence graph.

• Induction values are listed (canonically) in the order that their references first appear in the canonicalized control tree.

7 Matching Subprograms and Patterns

As discussed in greater details at the end of Sect. 2.2, we need to do the following in order to check whether a subprogram is an algorithmic instance of a pattern subprogram.

1. Compare the control flow structures of the subprograms.
2. Compare the conditions dominating the corresponding branches in the control flow structures.
3. Compare the corresponding simple statements.
4. Compare the corresponding i-vals.

The first three can be done by matching the control trees which are already in a canonical form. The last needs to be done using a different approach. This chapter explains how these matching processes work.

7.1 Matching Control Trees

After the control trees have been turned into a canonical form, matching them is a simple matter. We only need to do a simultaneous preorder traversal of both trees and compare the corresponding nodes. The details are given in Fig. 7.1.
The following theorem is obvious.

THEOREM 7.1: The time complexity of Algorithm $MatchingControlTrees$ is $O(|T_I|)$, where T_I is the control tree of the extracted subprogram. ∎

7.2 Matching Induction Values

Matching the i-vals of two subprograms involves three steps. The first step is to construct two i-val trees, one for each subprogram. Next the i-val trees are compared to make sure that they have the same tree shape. A system of integer **linear equations** is established in order to determine how the free variables of the pattern subprogram are substituted or renamed. The equations are set up by comparing the corresponding nodes that contain free variables. The last step is to check whether the system of integer linear equations has a unique solution. If it does, then find the solution if one exists. This solution will serve as part of the constraints under which the extracted subprogram matches the pattern subprogram.

Procedure $MatchingControlTrees(T_P, T_I, M, constraints)$
Input:

1. T_P: the control tree (in canonical form) of a pattern subprogram
2. T_I: the control trees (in canonical form) of an extracted subprogram

Output:

1. M: yes/no, and in case of yes
2. $constraints$: an array of records recording how the variables of T_P are renamed to match the variables of T_I.

Process:

Perform simultaneous preorder traversal of T_P and T_I, comparing every pair of corresponding nodes visited. Let v_p in T_P and v_i in T_I be a pair of nodes being compared. For each node pair, do the following:

if node type of $v_1 \neq$ node type of v_2 **then**

$M = no$

return

else

Compare v_1 to v_2 according to the following cases.

case 1: For two constants (or two operators), check whether they represent the same constant value (or operator).

case 2: For two i-vals, check whether they have equal integer identifications, assigned to them when all the i-vals of the subprogram were listed in a canonical order. (Refer to Sect. 6.5 for details.)

case 3: For variables v_p and v_i:

    if (this is v_p's first occurrence) **then**

        Rename v_p to v_i.

        Record the renaming of variables in array $constraints$. Check renaming consistency.

        Let TE_p and TE_i be the trees representing the type expressions for v_p and v_i, respectively.

        Simultaneously traverse both trees to check whether TE_i is an instantiation of type expression TE_p according to Def. 2.6. Record additional constraints in $constraints$. Check consistency as necessary.

    else

        if v_p has been renamed to v_i in $constraints$ **then**

            $M = yes$

        else

            $M = no$

        endif

    endif

endif

Figure 7.1
Algorithm to match control trees

Setting Up Equations by Comparing the I-val Trees

For example, consider a pattern subprogram containing a loop performing banded matrix computations in Fig. 7.2.

```
do j = 1,n
  do i = max(1,j-q+1), min(n,j+p-1)
    A(i,j) = ...
  enddo
enddo
```

Figure 7.2
Banded matrix loop — pattern subprogram

We have two i-vals (listed in a canonical order)

$?I_1 : (1, n, 1)$

$?I_2 : (\max(1, ?I_1 + 1 - q)), \min(n, ?I_1 + p - 1), 1).$

Now consider an extracted subprogram containing a loop performing banded matrix computations in Fig. 7.3.

```
DO I = 1,k
  DO J = max(1,I-9), min(k,I+3)
    X(J,I) = ...
  ENDDO
ENDDO
```

Figure 7.3
Banded matrix loop — extracted subprogram

The two i-vals are (listed in a canonical order)

$?I_1 : (1, k, 1)$

$?I_2 : (\max(1, ?I_1 - 9), \min(k, ?I_1 + 3), 1)$

The i-val trees for both the pattern and the extracted subprogram subprograms are shown in Fig. 7.4 and Fig. 7.5.

For the extracted subprogram to match the pattern subprogram, their i-val trees should have the same shape. Except for the highlighted nodes in the pattern i-val tree, all the corresponding nodes should match exactly. These nodes are selected because they contain

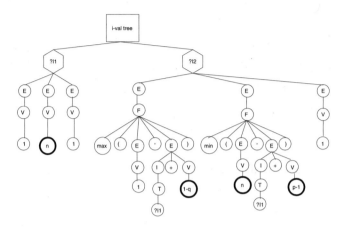

Figure 7.4
I-val trees for the pattern subprogram

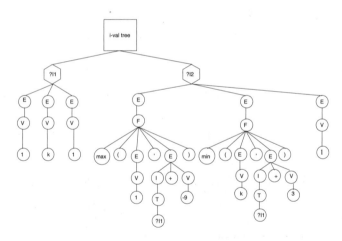

Figure 7.5
I-val trees for the extracted subprogram

non-constant expressions of free variables. For each high-lighted node in the pattern, an
equation is set up. So we have the following.

$$\begin{cases} n = k \\ 1 - q = 9 \\ n = k \\ p - 1 = 3 \end{cases} \qquad (7.1)$$

In the equations, the variables on the left side are the free variables from the pattern. The ones on the right are the free variables from the extracted subprogram. The equations are considered to have a solution if the variables on the left-hand side can be expressed in terms of a **multilinear expression** with integer coefficients of the variables on the right-hand side. If the equations have a solution, then we will have found a match between the i-vals of the extracted subprogram and the i-vals of the pattern subprogram.

For implementation purposes, an i-val tree can be represented in a much simpler form. The equations will be represented using matrixes and vectors. Assume the following.

- In the pattern i-val tree, there are n free variables $x_1, x_2, ..., x_n$.

- There are m nodes representing multilinear expressions of the free variables (the highlighted nodes in the example).

- In the extracted subprogram i-val tree, there are l free variables $y_1, y_2, ..., y_l$.

We have a system of m equations.

$$\begin{cases} a_{11}x_1 + a_{12}x_2 + ... + a_{1n}x_n + d_1 = b_{11}y_1 + b_{12}y_2 + ... + b_{1l}y_l + d_1' \\ a_{21}x_1 + a_{22}x_2 + ... + a_{2n}x_n + d_2 = b_{21}y_1 + b_{22}y_2 + ... + b_{2l}y_l + d_2' \\ ...... \\ a_{m1}x_1 + a_{m2}x_2 + ... + a_{mn}x_n + d_m = b_{m1}y_1 + b_{m2}y_2 + ... + b_{ml}y_l + d_m' \end{cases} \tag{7.2}$$

The system can be represented by integer matrixes as

$$A(m, n) \cdot x(n) = B(m, l) \cdot y(l) + (D'(m) - D(m)) \tag{7.3}$$

where $D(i) = d_i$ and $D'(i) = d_i'$ (for $i = 1, ..., m$), $A(i, j) = a_{ij}$ and $B(i, k) = B_{ik}$ (for $i = 1, ..., m$, $j = 1, ..., n$, and $k = 1, ..., l$).

Solving the Integer Equations

We now discuss how to solve the equations. Assume $m \geq n$, meaning that there are at least as many equations as the unknowns. Also assume $rank(A(m, n)) = n$. These two assumptions are important. Otherwise, the system may have more than one solution, implying that the free variables in pattern may not be independent of each other. In this case, we must fix the pattern first. We look for a unique integer solution in which each x_i ($1 \leq i \leq n$) will be expressed in terms of a **linear expression** of the y's with integer coefficients and integer constant factor.

To solve the system of equations, we compute an integer matrix $A'(m, m)$ such that,

$$A'(m, m) \cdot A(m, n) = W(m, n) = \begin{pmatrix} w_1 & & & \\ & w_2 & & \\ & & \ddots & \\ & & & w_n \\ 0 & 0 & \cdots & 0 \\ \vdots & \vdots & \ddots & \vdots \\ 0 & 0 & \cdots & 0 \end{pmatrix} \quad (7.4)$$

where w_i (for $i = 1, ..., n$) are non-zero integers. For the system of equations to have a unique solution, the last $m - n$ rows of both $A'(m, m) \cdot B(m, l)$ and $A'(m, m) \cdot (D'(m) - D(m))$ must all be zeros. Formally, we have the following integer matrix and integer vector.

$$A'(m, m) \cdot B(m, l) = \begin{pmatrix} p_{11} & p_{12} & \cdots & p_{1l} \\ p_{21} & p_{22} & \cdots & p_{2l} \\ \vdots & \vdots & \ddots & \vdots \\ p_{n1} & p_{n2} & \cdots & p_{nl} \\ 0 & 0 & \cdots & 0 \\ \vdots & \vdots & \ddots & \vdots \\ 0 & 0 & \cdots & 0 \end{pmatrix} \quad (7.5)$$

$$A'(m, m) \cdot (D'(m) - D(m)) = \begin{pmatrix} q_1 \\ q_2 \\ \vdots \\ q_n \\ 0 \\ \vdots \\ 0 \end{pmatrix} \quad (7.6)$$

The solution can be expressed as the following.

$$
\begin{pmatrix} x_1 \\ x_2 \\ \vdots \\ x_n \\ 0 \\ \vdots \\ 0 \end{pmatrix} = \begin{pmatrix} \frac{p_{11}}{w_1} & \frac{p_{12}}{w_1} & \cdots & \frac{p_{1l}}{w_1} \\ \frac{p_{21}}{w_2} & \frac{p_{22}}{w_2} & \cdots & \frac{p_{2l}}{w_2} \\ \vdots & \vdots & \ddots & \vdots \\ \frac{p_{n1}}{w_n} & \frac{p_{n2}}{w_n} & \cdots & \frac{p_{nl}}{w_n} \\ 0 & 0 & \cdots & 0 \\ \vdots & \vdots & \ddots & \vdots \\ 0 & 0 & \cdots & 0 \end{pmatrix} \cdot \begin{pmatrix} y_1 \\ y_2 \\ \vdots \\ y_l \end{pmatrix} + \begin{pmatrix} \frac{q_1}{w_1} \\ \frac{q_2}{w_2} \\ \vdots \\ \frac{q_n}{w_n} \\ 0 \\ \vdots \\ 0 \end{pmatrix} \tag{7.7}
$$

Furthermore, for the system of equations to have an integer solution, the above coefficient matrix and the constant vector must have integer elements only.

We now discuss how to compute $A'(m, m)$ from $A(m, n)$. The method we use is a special version of the **Gauss-Jordan elimination**. We start with a column augmented matrix $(A(m, n) \sqcup I(m, m))$.

$$
\left(\begin{pmatrix} a_{11} & a_{12} & \cdots & a_{1l} \\ a_{21} & a_{22} & \cdots & a_{2l} \\ \vdots & \vdots & \ddots & \vdots \\ a_{n1} & a_{n2} & \cdots & a_{nl} \\ \vdots & \vdots & \ddots & \vdots \\ a_{m1} & a_{m2} & \cdots & a_{ml} \end{pmatrix} \sqcup \begin{pmatrix} 1 & & & & \\ & 1 & & & \\ & & \ddots & & \\ & & & 1 & \\ & & & & \ddots \\ & & & & & 1 \end{pmatrix} \right) \tag{7.8}
$$

where the operator $\sqcup$ just signifies column augmentation, that is, removing the abutting parentheses and making a wider matrix out the operands of the $\sqcup$ operator. We perform simultaneous row operations on both $A(m, n)$ and $I(m, m)$. When $A(m, n)$ is turned into $W(m, n)$, matrix $I(m, m)$ will be turned into $A'(m, m)$. The row operations are the following:

- Interchange any two rows, and

- replace a row by a **linear combination** with integer weights of itself and any other rows.

For example, in order to eliminate all the elements but a_{11} in the first column, the right amount of the first row is subtracted from each other row. Using the standard approach (Gauss-Jordan elimination), this "right amount" is $\frac{a_{i1}}{a_{11}}$ for row i. However, this may result in non-integer elements. To overcome this, we can first multiply row i by

$\frac{LeastCommonMultiple(a_{i1},a_{11})}{a_{i1}}$, and then subtract from row i a right amount of the first row. Obviously, the right amount here is $\frac{LeastCommonMultiple(a_{i1},a_{11})}{a_{11}}$.

The following lemma is obvious.

LEMMA 7.1:   The equation system Eqn. 7.2 can be solved in $O(m^2 \times l)$ time.   ■

Therefore, we have the following theorem.

THEOREM 7.2:   Given a pattern subprogram and an extracted subprogram, their i-vals can be compared in $O(m^2 \times l)$ time, where m is the number of i-vals of the pattern subprogram that contain free variables, and l is the number of free variables in the i-vals of the extracted subprogram.   ■

For efficiency of the on-line pattern matching process, we can precompute matrix $D(m)$, $A(m,n)$ and further on $A'(m,m)$ and $W(m,n)$ for each pattern in the pattern database. This precomputation can be done off-line and needs to be done only once. With $D(m)$, $A'(m,m)$ and $W(m,n)$ available for the pattern, solving the equation system for an extracted subprogram becomes a matter of matrix multiplications $A'(m,m) \cdot B(m,l)$ and $A'(m,m) \cdot (D'(m) - D(m))$, and dividing the rows of the resultant matrixes by the first n diagonal elements of $W(m,n)$. For implementation purposes, $W(m,n)$ can be represented by a vector $w(n)$ that stores the non-zero diagonal elements of $W(m,n)$.

7.3   Constraint Consistency

As specified in Def. 2.7 and demonstrated in Fig. 2.8, it is necessary to maintain the consistency of constraints. Variables should be renamed one-to-one. For this purpose, an array of records called *constraints* records, during the matching process, how variables in the pattern are renamed and/or substituted. This array is consulted and updated when matching the control trees (Sect. 7.1), when matching the i-val trees (Sect. 7.2), and after solving the integer linear equation system (Sect. 7.2).

7.4   Speeding up Pattern Matching

There are ways to speed up the on-line pattern matching process. In this section, we discuss some of them.

Indexing the Patterns by Simple Invariants

The cost of turning a control tree into a canonical form and comparing it node by node with a pattern control tree cannot be ignored. We can avoid this cost by first using a few of the tree's **invariants** to match against those of the patterns.

This should be able to narrow down the range of patterns to match. The simple control tree invariants are the following:

- number of interior nodes,
- number of leaf nodes,
- number of array references,
- number of scalar variable references,
- number of additive operators,
- number of multiplicative operators,
- number of boolean operators,
- number of relational operators, and
- number of intrinsic procedure calls.

We can create similar invariants for the i-val tree, if they exist and are useful. We can build an index for all the patterns based on these invariants. To see the idea, consider an example in which we only use the first three invariants listed above. Represented by tuples of integers, assume the invariants for the patterns are the following:

- $T_1 : (100, 11, 10)$
- $T_2 : (49, 7, 9)$
- $T_3 : (49, 8, 5)$
- $T_4 : (49, 8, 6)$
- $T_5 : (85, 10, 10)$
- $T_6 : (100, 12, 10)$
- $T_7 : (49, 7, 10)$
- $T_8 : (85, 10, 11)$
- $T_9 : (100, 12, 10)$
- $T_{10} : (85, 10, 13)$
- $T_{11} : (49, 7, 6)$
- $T_{12} : (200, 15, 14)$
- $T_{13} : (100, 12, 10)$

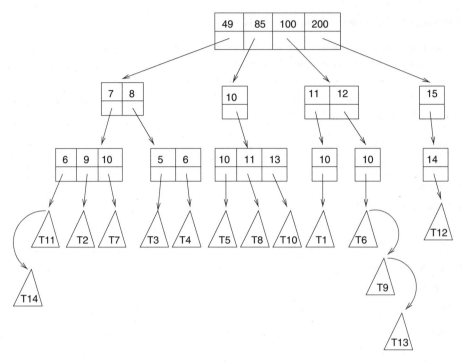

Figure 7.6
An example of the pattern database index structure

- $T_{14} : (49, 7, 6)$

This index is shown in Fig. 7.6.

The numbers in each rectangular box are sorted. This can be implemented by a sorted array or a binary search tree, which is more efficient for updating. Because the update of the pattern database and the index structure can be done off-line, a simple array implementation is preferable.

In the worst case, on-line searching using such an indexing structure can be done in $O(\log L)$ time, where L is the number of patterns in the pattern database.

In our approach, the indexing is done off-line. Thus, we can always derive invariants that are so strong that only a bounded constant number of patterns may share all the same invariants. See App. D for data that supports this assertion.

Preprocessing the Patterns in the Data Base

Before the on-line pattern matching begins, all the patterns in the database can be preprocessed. For a pattern subprogram, the preprocessing includes the following.

- Turn its control tree into a canonical form (Chap. 6).
- Set up the i-val tree (Sect. 6.5).
- Precompute the matrices of the integer equation solver needed for matching the i-vals as discussed towards the end of Sect. 7.2.

7.5 Summary

- Matching the control trees in canonical forms can be done by simultaneous traversals of both trees.
- Matching i-vals involves comparing i-val trees, creating a system of linear equations that relate variables in the extracted subprogram and the pattern, and solving that system.
- We use a special version of Gauss-Jordan elimination to obtain an integer solution to the equation system.
- Much of the computation of the equations can be done off-line.
- Patterns are indexed by invariants of their trees to provide rapid database lookup. The number of patterns thus found is always bounded by a small constant.

8 Extracting Subprograms

In this chapter we discuss how to extract statements, from the computational kernel, to form as extracted subprograms to match against the algorithm patterns. Eventually, we want to be able to replace these statements with a library procedure call.

For replacement, the statements to be extracted together should be executed under the same control flow conditions in the computational kernel. Given the control tree as the internal representation for the computational kernel, we only need to consider multiple statements that are the children of the same control-group node, or a single statement. Extracting a single statement is straightforward. Extracting some of the statements under a control-group node is far from trivial if the extracted statements together need to have the potential to match one of the patterns.

8.1 Statement Extraction Heuristics

Which statements together can have potential to match one of the algorithm patterns depends on what the patterns are. A computational kernel may include several different algorithms. In control tree representation, all the statements of the top control flow level are represented as children of the root, a control-group node. An arbitrary combination of these top level statements may not make up a meaningful algorithm. In order for the extracted statements to form a meaningful algorithm, the group of statements together should meet certain necessary conditions.

DEFINITION 8.1:

Computational Confluence: A group of statements is computationally confluent, if the group contains only one loop statement, or if the group contains multiple statements and the following conditions are true:

(A) The statements are executed under the same control flow. In the control tree representation, they are children of the same control-group node v.

(B) Let G be the statement-level data flow dependence graph on all the children of v. Each member of the group is connected to at least one other member, through a true data flow dependence arc in G.

(C) Each strongly connected component in G is either completely included in the group or completely outside the group.

(D) At least one of the statements is a loop.

∎

Condition (B) focuses our attention on statements among which there is computational dependence. Based on experience, Condition (C) is introduced for two reasons. First, it is unlikely that a meaningful algorithm is formed by mixing some of the statements in a strongly connected component with others outside the component. Second, a subset consisting of two or more statements from a strongly connected component is unlikely to make up a meaningful algorithm. Condition (D) reflects the fact that we are only interested in optimizing subprograms containing loops. Conditions (B)–(D) describe, in G, the topology and the types of arcs and nodes of the subgraph we are interested in.

Consider the code in Fig. 8.1, which was introduced in Chap. 1. There are severally groups of computationally confluent code here. Statements 3–6 are connected to each other through the data dependence on the variable s. The strongly connected region in statement 5 is included entirely within the group. There is a cycle from this statement to itself due to dependencies connecting the references to s. They are all executed under the same control flow conditions, and statements 4–6 comprise a complete loop.

Another computationally confluent group is formed by adding statement 7 to the previous group. The data flow connection is again through the variable s. Finally, the entire code segment is yet another computationally confluent group of statements.

```
002     do j=1,k-1
003       s=a(j,k)
004       do i=j+1,n
005         s=s+a(i,j)*a(i,k)
006       end do
007       s=s*h(j)
008       a(j,k)=a(j,k)+s
009       do i=j+1,n
010         a(i,k)=a(i,k)+s*a(i,j)
011       end do
012     end do
```

Figure 8.1
Computationally confluent code

The algorithm to extract all the subprograms consisting of computationally confluent groups of statements, is presented in Fig. 8.2. First, we will define some additional notation.

DEFINITION 8.2: **Induced Subgraph:** Let $G = (V, E)$ be a graph. A graph $G' = (V', E')$ is an induced subgraph of G if $V' \subseteq V$ and $E' = \{(v_1, v_2) \in E | v_1, v_2 \in V'\}$. We say G' is a subgraph of G induced by V'. ■

DEFINITION 8.3: **Connected Component:** Let $G = (V, E)$ be an undirected graph. Two vertices u and w are connected if there is a path from u to w. u and w are directly connected if $(u, w) \in E$. A connected component (undirected) is a subset $V' \subseteq V$ such that the vertices in V' are connected. Define the distance between u and w, $distance(u, w)$, as the number of arcs in the shortest path from u to w. ∎

Later in the chaper, we discuss the computational complexity of Procedure $Extract Subprograms For Matching$

8.2   Computing Connected Components

The idea of the algorithm to list all the connected components of an undirected graph is as follows. Standing at a vertex v, all the vertices in the undirected graph G can be seen as belonging to layers, according to their distance from v. Those not connected to v have an infinite distance from v. They belong to a layer of their own. To find all the connected components, the algorithm takes combinations of the subsets of layers, from inner layers out. The algorithm makes use of stacks to make the combinations.

At the beginning, the component contains only v, placed in a stack called $Stack Of Selected$. As a second step, any combination of the candidate vertices directly connected to v can be added to make up a larger connected component. We want to make sure all such combinations of the candidates will eventually be considered. Thus, we record the list of candidates available at this point in a different stack called $Stack Of Candidates$. In other words, the vertices in $Stack Of Candidates[1]$ all have a distance 1 (one) from vertex v.

To enlarge incrementally the connected component, a new combination of the candidate vertices are added. This combination is also pushed onto $Stack Of Selected$. Meanwhile, new candidates become available, which were not directly connected to the old members of the component, but are directly connected to the new members. The new list of of candidates is pushed onto $Stack Of Candidates$. We pop off the top elements from the stacks when all combinations of the candidates at the top of $Stack Of Candidates$ have been considered. To remember the number of combinations not yet considered, we maintain a third stack of integers. This goes on until the stacks become empty.

There are two invariants in the algorithm:

(1) The vertices in $Stack Of Candidates[k]$ ($1 \leq k \leq top$) all have a distance k from vertex v.

(2) $Stack Of Selected[k + 1] \subseteq Stack Of Candidates[k]$.

In the algorithm, we need to be able to list all the subsets (combinations) of a given set.

Procedure *ExtractSubprogramsForMatching*(*T*, *DF*)
Input:

1. *T*: A control tree representing the whole computational kernel.
2. *DF*: The statement-level data-flow dependence graphs for *T*.

Output:

1. All subprograms, each consisting of a group of statements that are "computationally confluent" (Def. 8.1).

Process:

Compute and record the simple control tree invariants of each subtree of *T*. /* We do this here to speed up computing the invariants of subprograms extracted from *T* */

Traverse *T* and do the following upon visiting a node *v*:

if (*v* is a loop whose parent in *T* is not a control-group node) **then**

Create a new control tree *T'* with *v* being its only top level statement hanging under the root (of *T'*), a control-group node.

For each control-group node in *T'*, construct a statement-level data flow dependence graph for its children. (The data flow dependence graphs for *T'* can be obtained from those for *T*.)

Record *T'*, its statement-level data flow dependence graphs, and its i-vals, on output list.

else if (*v* is a control-group node) **then**

Let *G'* be the statement-level data flow dependence graph on the children of *v*.

Construct an undirected graph *G* from *G'* as follows. Each node in *G* represents either a strongly connected component in *G'* or a single node in *G'* not belonging to any strongly connected component. Each node of *G* remembers the group of nodes of *G'* it represents. Make an arc between v_1 and v_2 of *G* if there exists a TRUE data flow dependence arc in *G'* between the groups they represent.

for (each vertex *w* of *G* representing a loop) **do**

    call *AllConnectedInducedSubgraphVertexSets*(*G*, *w*)

    for each connected component *U* **do**

        Assume $s_1, s_2, ..., s_k$ are the vertices (statements) in *U*, listed in the same order as in *T*.

        Create a new control tree *T'* with $s_1, s_2, ..., s_k$ being the top level statements as the children of the root, which is a new control-group node.

        For each control-group node in *T'*, construct a statement-level data flow dependence graph for its children. The statement-level data flow dependence graph for the top level statements of *T'* is just the subgraph of *G'* induced by *U*.

        Compute the control tree invariants of *T'* from those of *T*.

        end

    end

endif

Figure 8.2
Algorithm to extract subprograms for matching

Consider a set $S = \{v_1, v_2, ..., v_k\}$. There are a total of $2^k - 1$ non-empty subsets of *S*. One way to list and rank its subsets is to represent each subset by a *k*-bit binary number. For

$1 \leq j \leq k$, the j-th bit being 1/0 indicates whether v_j is or isn't in the subset. The value of the binary number is used as the rank of the subset. Formally, the algorithm is given in Fig. 8.3.

Whenever $top > 0$, the union U of the sets in $StackOfSelected$ form a connected component containing v. $StackOfCandidates[top]$ is the set of vertices that are directly connected to the vertices in set $StackOfSelected[top]$, but not to the vertices of U. $StackOfSubsetNum[top]$ remembers the number of subsets (combinations) of $StackOfCandidates[top]$ that have yet to be considered.

THEOREM 8.1:   Algorithm $AllConnectedInducedSubgraphVertexSets()$ is optimal

Proof. To argue about the correctness of the algorithm, we need to show that any connected component containing v will be generated by the algorithm at some point. Consider connected component V containing v. It is sufficient to show that V will be generated by the algorithm. For this purpose, we partition V into m disjoint subset V_0, V_1, ..., V_m such that

- $V_0 = \{v\}$,
- V_1 contains all the vertices in V that are directly connected to v.
- V_2 contains all the vertices in V that are directly connected to some of vertices in V_1, but not directly connected to v.
- V_j ($2 \leq j \leq m$) contains all the vertices in V that are directly connected to some of vertices in V_{j-1}, but not directly connected to the vertices in any of V_i ($i = 1, ..., j-2$).

Now, we only need to show that there is a time when V_0, V_1, ..., V_m are the only items in stack $StackOfSelected$. We can prove this by induction. As the induction basis, it is obvious that V_0 is pushed onto the stack at the beginning of the algorithm. Assume that for any $j < m$, there is a time when V_0, V_1, ..., V_j are the only items in $StackOfSelected$. We want to show V_{j+1} will at some time be pushed on top of V_j. This is obvious because every vertex in V_{j+1} is a candidate vertex in set $StackOfCandidates[j]$. V_{j+1} is just one combination of candidates. Therefore V_{j+1} will be pushed on top of V_j at some point.

Let us consider the complexity of the algorithm. The algorithm outputs a connected component every time a new item is pushed onto $StackOfSelected$. It is obvious that the algorithm never outputs the same connected component twice. So the number of push operations is equal to the number of possible connected components. The same is true for the number of pop operations. Consequently, the number of iterations of the while-loop is the same as the number of possible connected components. The computation of U is part of the output process. The time to compute s_1 in all steps together will not exceed the time

---

Procedure $AllConnectedInducedSubgraphVertexSets(G, v)$
Input:

1. G: an undirected graph,
2. v: a vertex of G

Output:

1. the vertex sets of all the connected component containing vertex v.

Variables:

1. $StackOfSelected$: a stack where each item is a set of vertices.
2. $StackOfCandidates$: a stack where each item is also a set of vertices.
3. $StackOfSubsetNum$: a stack where each item is an integer.
4. s_1, s_2, I, top

Process:

Precompute the distance from v for every vertex of G;
$top = 1$;
$s_1 = \{v\}$;
$StackOfSelected[top] = s_1$;
Output $\{v\}$;
$s_2 = \{w | (v, w) \text{ is an arc}\}$;
$StackOfCandidates[top] = s_2$;
$StackOfSubsetNum[top] = 2^{|s_2|} - 1$;
while $(top > 0)$ **do**
$I = StackOfSubsetNum[top]$;
$StackOfSubsetNum[top] = StackOfSubsetNum[top] - 1$;
if $(I > 0)$ **then**
    s_1 = the I-th subset of set $StackOfCandidates[top]$;
    $top = top + 1$;
    $StackOfSelected[top] = s_1$;
    $U = StackOfSelected[1] \bigcup ... \bigcup StackOfSelected[top]$;
    Output U;
    $s_2 = \{w | \text{ distance(v,w)} = top, \text{ and there is an arc } (u, w) \text{ with } u \in s_1\}$;
    $StackOfCandidates[top] = s_2$;
    $StackOfSubsetNum[top] = 2^{|s_2|} - 1$;
else
    $top = top - 1$;
endif
end

Figure 8.3
Algorithm to find all connected induced subgraph vertex sets

required to compute U. This is also true of the total time to compute s_2 in all the steps, if we pre-arrange all the vertices by their distances to v. Therefore the algorithm is optimal. ∎

THEOREM 8.2:   Algorithm *Extract Subprograms For Matching* computes all computationally confluent groups of statements in optimal time.

Proof. It is easy to see that the algorithm computes exactly all computationally confluent groups of statements. The time complexity optimality relies on that of Algorithm *AllConnectedInducedSubgraphVertexSets()*, presented in Sect. 8.2. ∎

8.3   The Worst Case

Algorithm *ExtractSubprogramsForMatching* is optimal in the sense that its time complexity is proportional to the number of computationally confluent groups of statements it returns. For a control-group node with k children statements, there are 2^k possible ways to group the children. Theoretically, however, the number of computationally confluent groups could be as many as 2^{k-1}, as shown in the following example. All k statements in the example are children of the same top level control-group node. Any grouping of them including S1 is considered computationally confluent according to Def. 8.1. There are 2^{k-1} such groups.

```
S1:   do i = ...
         A = A+ ...
      enddo
S2:   ... use variable ''A'' ...
      ...
Sk:   ... use variable ''A'' ...
```

In practice, the number of children statements of a control-group node tends to be small, especially in such a case as this example. Besides, many of these computationally confluent groups as extracted subprograms will be rejected by just checking the simple program invariants as discussed in Sect. 7.4.

Our approach to extract extracted subprograms is a heuristic based on Def. 8.1. Improvement is possible if we could find a better criterion of being "computationally confluent."

8.4 Summary

• We extract groups of statements for analysis based on the node types, arc types, and topology of the data dependence graph.

• The patterns in the database all contain loops, so for a subprogram to be computationally confluent, it must contain a loop.

• The anti- and output- dependencies in the graph reflect the artifact of memory, and so are not used to find related computations.

• Taking some statements from a strongly connected region (SCR) eliminates a basic relationship of sequencing, so SCR's are treated as a unit.

9 Valid Algorithm Replacement

After pattern matching, many different groups of statements (as subprograms) of the computational kernel could be found to match the algorithm patterns. When a group of statements matches an algorithm pattern, it may be possible to replace this group of statements in the computational kernel with a library procedure call that is semantically equivalent. An **algorithm replacement** carries out such a replacement. When we talk about the algorithm replacement, we always imply that the replacing procedure call is semantically equivalent to the subprogram consisting of the statements to be replaced.

An algorithm replacement involving a single statement is always valid. An algorithm replacement involving multiple statements, however, is not always valid.

DEFINITION 9.1:   **Valid Replacement:** Such a replacement is valid if two conditions are fulfilled

- The subprogram consisting of the statements to be replaced is semantically equivalent to the library procedure being called, with the appropriate parameters.
- There is a valid statement ordering according to the semantics of the source program, in which the statements to be replaced are listed next to each other.

The first part is determined by algorithmic instance testing. A necessary and sufficient condition is given for the second in this chapter.

Even if each algorithm replacement is valid when applied alone on the computational kernel, performing several such replacements simultaneously could be invalid for two reasons.

- The replacements may overlap.
- There exists no valid statement ordering for the statements in each group to be placed contiguously.

In this chapter, we give a necessary and sufficient condition under which it is valid to apply one or more algorithm replacements. The condition is given in terms of a topological property of the statement-level data flow dependence graphs. Consequently, we are able to give an algorithm, which has time complexity linear to the size of the graphs, to test whether this condition is satisfied.

In the presentation, we shall use T for the control tree representing the computational kernel we want to optimize. When no confusion is possible, we sometimes use a set of nodes in T to stand for a replacement. For a replacement r, such a set contains exactly the roots of the subtrees representing the statements. We say that the replacement can occur at these nodes, which are roots of the subtrees.

9.1 More on Statement Order and Data Flow Dependences

Whether a group of statements can be replaced by a semantically equivalent library procedure call depends on how the statements can be reordered without violating the semantics of the program. As discussed in Sect. 6.4, for the children statements of a control-group node in the control tree, the valid ordering of these statements is constrained by the statement-level data flow dependence graph G. (Refer to Sect. 5.6 for its definition.) If G is acyclic, then any topological order of the statements is valid. If G is cyclic, then, in any valid statement ordering, statements belonging to the same strongly connected component of G are listed in the same relative order as in the source program. Statements belonging to different strongly connected components are listed according to the dependence constraints of G.

In Sect. 6.4, we introduced the concept of vertex collapsing. We also gave some examples. Here, we shall discuss more of the relationship between vertex collapsing and valid statement ordering. For example, collapsing a set of vertices in an acyclic directed graph may introduce directed cycles in the resultant graph. As another example, consider the graph in Fig. 9.1. Collapsing only $\{1, 2, 3\}$ or $\{4, 5, 6\}$ will not introduce any cycles. However, collapsing both $\{1, 2, 3\}$ and $\{4, 5, 6\}$ will make the resultant graph cyclic.

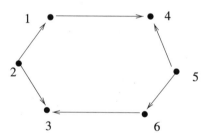

Figure 9.1
Collapsing vertices of a directed acyclic graph may introduce directed cycles

DEFINITION 9.2: **Simultaneously Collapsible:** Let G be a directed graph. Let V_1, V_2, ..., V_k be disjoint multi-element subsets of the vertices in G such that, for every strongly connected component S (of G) and each V_i $(1 \leq i \leq k)$, we have either $S \subseteq V_i$ or

$S \cap V_i = \Phi$. We say V_1, V_2, ..., V_k are simultaneously collapsible if simultaneously collapsing all the V_i (for $i = 1, ..., k$) as well as all the strongly connected components not included in any V_i results in an acyclic graph. ∎

THEOREM 9.1:   Let V be a set of all the children statements of a control-group node on T. Let G be the statement-level data flow dependence graph on V. Let V_1, V_2, ..., V_k be disjoint multi-element subsets of V such that, for every strongly connected component S (of G) and each V_i ($1 \leq i \leq k$), we have either $S \subseteq V_i$ or $S \cap V_i = \Phi$. There is a valid statement ordering that lists the members of each V_i ($1 \leq i \leq k$) together if and only if V_1, V_2, ..., V_k are simultaneously collapsible.

Proof. ("If" part) Assume that V_1, V_2, ..., V_k are simultaneously collapsible in graph G. Let G' be the acyclic directed graph resulting from collapsing all the V_i ($1 \leq i \leq k$) as well as all the strongly connected components that are not subsets of any V_i.

The valid statement ordering can be obtained by the following steps. (1) Perform a topological sort on G'. (2) Replace each vertex v' of G' in the topological sequence with the subset of vertices of G that v' represents. List the vertices in this subset according to their original order as in the source program.

("Only if" part) Given that there exists a valid statement ordering in which the vertices in each V_i ($1 \leq i \leq k$) are listed together, we need to show that the graph G' constructed in the following steps is acyclic. (i) Collapse, one by one, all the strongly connected component S_1, ..., S_q, which are not subsets of any one of V_1, V_2, ..., V_k, and then, (ii) collapse V_1, V_2, ..., V_k one by one.

For a directed graph, collapsing any one of its strongly connected component into a single vertex w will not introduce any new cycle containing w in the resultant graph. So step (i) will not introduce any new cycle. Let us consider step (ii). Any valid statement ordering has to respect data flow dependencies. Thus, vertices of V_i ($1 \leq i \leq k$) being listed together in a valid statement ordering implies that, for any u_1 and u_2 in V_i, every directed path between u_1 and u_2 only goes through vertices inside V_i. Collapsing any of V_1, V_2, ..., V_k after step (i) will not introduce any new cycle. Step (ii) will not introduce any new cycle. After steps (i) and (ii), all the strongly connected components originally in G will have all been collapsed, so the resultant graph is acyclic. Therefore, V_1, V_2, ..., V_k are simultaneously collapsible. ∎

9.2 Feasible Replacements

PROPOSITION 9.1:   Applying a single algorithm replacement on the computational kernel is valid if and only if there is a valid statement ordering, according to the semantics of the program, in which the statements to be replaced are listed next to each other. ■

DEFINITION 9.3:   **Overlapping Replacements:** Two replacements are overlapping if the groups of statements that they replace overlap under either of the following circumstances.

- The groups share some common member.
- The statements in one group are parts (sub-statements) of a statement in the other group.

A set of replacements is said to be non-overlapping if the replacements are pair-wise non-overlapping. ■

Consider the code in Fig. 9.2, which was introduced in Chap. 1. This code is a loop wrapped around code that could be replaced by calls to the BLAS routines DDOT (lines 3–6) and DAXPY (lines 9–11). The replaced code segments do not share a common member, and are not a subset of each other. Hence, the replacements are not overlapping.

```
002     do j=1,k-1
003        s=a(j,k)
004        do i=j+1,n
005           s=s+a(i,j)*a(i,k)
006        end do
007        s=s*h(j)
008        a(j,k)=a(j,k)+s
009        do i=j+1,n
010           a(i,k)=a(i,k)+s*a(i,j)
011        end do
012     end do
```

Figure 9.2
Non-overlapping replacements code

It may not be possible (or valid) to apply an overlapping set of replacements to the computational kernel. We will focus our attention on the potential replacement sets that are non-overlapping.

DEFINITION 9.4:   **Feasible Replacements:** A set of replacements is said to be feasible if applying only the replacements in the set to the computational kernel does not violate the semantics. ■

Feasibility is related to the simultaneous application of a set of replacements, so it is more general than the concept of validity which is related to a single replacement alone.

PROPOSITION 9.2:   A non-overlapping set of algorithm replacements is feasible if and only if there is a valid statement ordering, according to the semantics of the program, in which the statements to be involved in the same replacement are listed together. Statements to be involved in different replacements may be apart.   ■

COROLLARY 9.1:   Let R be a set of algorithm replacements. Let r be an algorithm replacement involving only a single statement. If $R \bigcup \{r\}$ is non-overlapping, and R is feasible, then $R \bigcup \{r\}$ is feasible.   ■

By Prop. 9.2 and Thm. 9.1, we have the following theorem.

THEOREM 9.2:   Let v be a control-group node on T. Let V be the set of all children of v. Let G be the statement-level data flow dependence graph for the children of v. Let $R = \{r_1, r_2, ..., r_k\}$ be a non-overlapping set of algorithm replacements on the children of v, where each r_i ($1 \leq i \leq k$) is represented as a subset of V, satisfying the following two conditions. (1) Each r_i replaces multiple statements. (2) For each strongly connected component S of G, either $S \subseteq r_i$ or $S \bigcap r_i = \Phi$. R is feasible if and only if $r_1, r_2, ..., r_k$ are simultaneously collapsible in graph G.   ■

Theorem 9.2 gives a necessary and sufficient condition under which simultaneous application of a set of algorithm replacements on the children statements of the same node is valid.

THEOREM 9.3:   Let R be a non-overlapping set of algorithm replacements. R is feasible if and only if, for every subset $R' \subseteq R$ of replacements that can occur at the children of the same node in the control tree, R' is feasible.

Proof. Trivially, we can partition R into subsets of replacements such that all the replacements that can occur at the children of the same node are put into the same subset. Obviously, replacements in different subsets do not interfere. R is feasible if and only if all of these subsets are individually feasible.   ■

9.3 Testing the Feasibility of Replacements

Theorem 9.3 tells us that testing the feasibility of a non-overlapping set of algorithm replacements can be done by testing separately the feasibility of its subsets containing replacements that occur at the children of the same node in the control tree. Algorithm $FeasibleReplacement(R)$ is to test the feasibility of each such subset. The idea of $FeasibleReplacement(R)$ is based on Corollary 9.1, and Thm(s). 9.1 and 9.2. The algorithm is presented in Fig. 9.3.

Function $FeasibleReplacement(R)$
Input:

1. T: the control tree of the whole program.
2. v: a node in T.
3. V: the set containing all the children of v on T.
4. $G = (V, E)$: the statement-level data flow dependence graph on V.
5. R: $R = \{r_1, r_2, ..., r_k\}$ is a set of algorithm replacements that can occur at v's children in T. For each $r \in R$, r is represented as a subset of V, $r \subseteq V$. Also, if $|r| > 1$, then for each strongly connected component S of G we have either $S \subseteq r$ or $S \bigcap r = \Phi$

Output:

1. yes/no indicating whether R is feasible.

Process:

> **if** $(R = \Phi)$ **then**
> **return** yes;
>
> **if** $\left(\bigcap_{r \in R} r \neq \Phi \right)$ **then**
> **return** no;
> Find all the strongly connected components in G.
> Let $S_1, S_2, ..., S_q$ be all the strongly connected components which are not subsets of any $r_1, ..., r_k$; Collapse $S_1, S_2, ..., S_q, r_1, ..., r_k$. Let G' be the resultant graph.
> **if** $(G'$ is acyclic) **then**
> **return** yes;
> **return** no;

Figure 9.3
Algorithm to determine the feasibility of replacements

THEOREM 9.4:   The time complexity of Algorithm $Feasible()$ is $O(|E| + |V|)$.

Proof. The most expensive step in the algorithm is to compute all strongly connected components of G, which can be done in $O(|E| + |V|)$ time using Tarjan's algorithm (48). ∎

9.4 Summary

• Whether a group of statements can be replaced depends on the valid orderings of those statements.

• We limit our consideration to non-overlapping replacements.

10 Selecting Algorithm Replacements

Even if it is valid to apply simultaneously algorithm replacements to different parts of the computational kernel, different replacements may result in different improvements in performance.

In this chapter, we discuss how to select the feasible set (see Def. 9.4), of algorithm replacements to maximize the total performance improvements. Once again, in the presentation, we shall use T for the control tree representing the computational kernel we want to optimize. When no confusion is possible, we sometimes use a set of nodes in T to stand for a replacement. For a replacement r, such a set contains exactly the roots of the subtrees representing the statements. We say that the replacement can occur at these nodes, which are roots of the subtrees.

10.1 Selection of Replacements

DEFINITION 10.1: **Replacement Selection:** A selection of algorithm replacements is a set of algorithm replacements that is feasible. (Refer to Def. 9.4.) ■

In order to choose among all possible selections in T, it is necessary to know how great the savings are from each replacement. We assume, for replacement r, that there is a function $savings(r)$. The value of $savings(r)$ depends on the replacing library procedure call as well as the original statements. We will discuss later how to evaluate this function for each replacement.

Given a selection in T, the benefit is defined to be the total savings of the replacements. In particular, let S be a selection.

$$benefit(S, T) = \sum_{r \in S} savings(r) \tag{10.1}$$

Define another function $MaxBenefit(T)$ to be the maximum benefit that can be gained among all the selections in control tree T.

$$MaxBenefit(T) = \max_{\text{all selection } S \text{ in } T} \{benefit(S, T)\} \tag{10.2}$$

The **Replacement Selection Problem:** Find the selection S among all the selections in control tree T satisfying $benefit(S, T) = MaxBenefit(T)$. We call S the best selection on T.

10.2   A Recursive Formulation

Denote $subtree(v)$ as the subtree rooted at node v in T. Let r be a replacement. We say that r can occur inside $subtree(v)$ if r can occur at some nodes in $subtree(v)$, but not at node v. Let S be a selection of replacements. Define function $SubSelection()$, and extend functions $benefit()$, and $MaxBenefit()$ as follows.

$$SubSelection(S, subtree(v)) = \{r \in S \mid r \text{ can occur inside } subtree(v)\} \tag{10.3}$$

$$benefit(S, subtree(v)) = \sum_{r \in SubSelection(S, subtree(v))} savings(r) \tag{10.4}$$

$$MaxBenefit(subtree(v)) = \max_{\text{all selection } S \text{ in } T} \{benefit(S, subtree(v))\} \tag{10.5}$$

THEOREM 10.1:   Let v be a node in T. Let $R_v = \{r_1, r_2, ..., r_q\}$ be the set of all potential replacements that can occur at the children of v. Let $U = \{u_1, u_2, ..., u_k\}$ be the set of all the children of v. ($r \subseteq U$ for each $r \in R_v$.) For each $R \subseteq R_v$, define predicate $Feasible(R)$ as

$Feasible(R) : R$ is feasible.

Then, we have the following recursion.

$$MaxBenefit(subtree(v)) = \tag{10.6}$$

$$\max_{\substack{R \subseteq R_v \\ s.t. \\ Feasible(R)}} \left\{ \sum_{r \in R} savings(r) + \sum_{u \in (U - \bigcup_{r \in R} r)} MaxBenefit(subtree(u)) \right\}$$

Proof. For simplicity, we use $MB()$ to stand for function $MaxBenefit()$ throughout the proof. It is necessary and sufficient to prove two parts:

(a) For every selection S of replacements in T,

$$benefit(S, subtree(v)) \tag{10.7}$$

$$\leq \max_{\substack{R \subseteq R_v \\ s.t. \\ Feasible(R)}} \left\{ \sum_{r \in R} savings(r) + \sum_{u \in (U - \bigcup_{r \in R} r)} MB(subtree(u)) \right\}$$

(b) there exists such a selection S' of replacements in T that,

$$benefit(S', subtree(v)) \tag{10.8}$$

$$= \max_{\substack{R \subseteq R_v \\ s.t. \\ Feasible(R)}} \left\{ \sum_{r \in R} savings(r) + \sum_{u \in (U - \bigcup_{r \in R} r)} MB(subtree(u)) \right\}$$

Proof of (a). Let $R' = S \cap R_v$. Then we have,

$$benefit(S, subtree(v)) \tag{10.9}$$

$$= \sum_{r \in SubSelection(S, subtree(v))} savings(r)$$

$$= \sum_{r \in R'} savings(r) + \sum_{u \in \left(U - \bigcup_{r \in R'} r \right)} \left(\sum_{r \in SubSelection(S, subtree(u))} savings(r) \right)$$

$$= \sum_{r \in R'} savings(r) + \sum_{u \in \left(U - \bigcup_{r \in R'} r \right)} benefit(S, subtree(u))$$

$$\leq \sum_{r \in R'} savings(r) + \sum_{u \in \left(U - \bigcup_{r \in R'} r \right)} MB(subtree(u))$$

$$\leq \max_{\substack{R \subseteq R_v \\ s.t. \\ Feasible(R)}} \left\{ \sum_{r \in R} savings(r) + \sum_{u \in \left(U - \bigcup_{r \in R} r\right)} MB(subtree(u)) \right\}$$

Proof of (b). We prove (b) by showing how to construct S' such that Eqn.(10.8) holds.

Let $R'' \subseteq R_v$ be the feasible set of replacements that maximizes the right hand side of Eqn.(10.6). That is,

$$\left(\sum_{r \in R''} savings(r) + \sum_{u \in (U - \bigcup_{r \in R''} r)} MB(subtree(u)) \right)$$

$$\equiv \max_{\substack{R \subseteq R_v \\ s.t. \\ Feasible(R)}} \left\{ \sum_{r \in R} savings(r) + \sum_{u \in (U - \bigcup_{r \in R} r)} MB(subtree(u)) \right\}$$

For each $u \in (U - \bigcup_{r \in R''})$, let $S(u)$ be the feasible set of replacements that maximizes the total savings in $subtree(u)$, that is, $\sum_{r \in S(u)} savings(r) = MB(subtree(u))$. Construct S' as the following.

$$S' = R'' \bigcup \left(\bigcup_{u \in \left(U - \bigcup_{r \in R''}\right)} S(u) \right) \tag{10.10}$$

By Thm. 9.3, S' is feasible. Furthermore,

$$benefit(S', subtree(v)) \tag{10.11}$$
$$= \sum_{r \in SubSelection(S', subtree(v))} savings(r)$$

$$= \sum_{r \in R''} savings(r) + \sum_{u \in (U - \bigcup_{r \in R''})} \left(\sum_{r \in S(u)} savings(r) \right)$$

$$= \sum_{r \in R''} savings(r) + \sum_{u \in (U - \bigcup_{r \in R''})} MB(subtree(u))$$

$$= \max_{\substack{R \subseteq R_v \\ s.t. \\ Feasible(R)}} \left\{ \sum_{r \in R} savings(r) + \sum_{u \in \left(U - \bigcup_{r \in R} r\right)} MB(subtree(u)) \right\}$$

∎

10.3   A Replacement Selection Algorithm

Based on Thm. 10.1, Fig. 10.1 presents a recursive algorithm to find the selection that maximizes the benefit in each subtree. Symbolic manipulation may be necessary to compare the benefits of different selections. This can happen when the value of $savings(r)$ is given, for example, as an expression of some input variables in the computational kernel.

To compute the best selection S on T, we just need to invoke this function by $MaximizeBenefit(root_T, S)$.

THEOREM 10.2:   The time complexity of Algorithm $MB(root_T)$ is

$$O \left(\sum_{v \text{ in } T} \left((|E_v| + |V_v|) \times 2^{|R_v|} \right) \right),$$ where $root_T$ is the root of the control tree T

representing the whole computational kernel being optimized. (E_v, V_v) represents the statement-level data flow dependence graph on the children statements of node v in T.

Proof. Algorithm $MB()$ is recursive based on the recursion in Thm. 10.1. To see its time complexity, we should analyze how much time is spent on each node v. Let R_v be all the potential algorithm replacements that can occur at the children of v. Let $G_v = (V_v, E_v)$ be the statement-level data flow dependence graph on v's children statements. The algorithm enumerates all possible subsets of R_v. For each subset $R \subseteq R_v$,

---

Function $MaximizeBenefit(v, S)$
Input:

1. v: a node in T, the control tree of the whole program.
2. R_v: the set of all potential replacements that can occur at the children of v.
3. $savings(r)$: the potential savings for every potential replacement r.

Output:

1. S: a feasible set of replacements inside $subtree(v)$ such that

$$\sum_{r \in S} savings(r) = MaxBenefit(v)$$

We use a set of sibling nodes in T to stand for a replacement.

Variables: $MB, MBTemp, STemp, STemp1, U, U'$. **Process:**

$MB = 0$;
$S = \Phi$;
$U = \{\text{all children of } v\}$;
if (v is a leaf, or there are no replacements inside $subtree(v)$) **then**
return MB;
for (each $R \subseteq R_v$) **do** /* $R \subseteq R_v$ includes the case $R = \Phi$ */
if ($Feasible(R)$) **then**
$\quad U' = U - \bigcup_{r \in R} r$;
$\quad MBTemp = 0$;
$\quad STemp = R$;
$\quad$ **for** (each $r \in R$) **do**
$\qquad MBTemp = MBTemp + savings(r)$
$\quad$ **for** (each $u \in U'$) **do**
$\qquad MBTemp = MBTemp + MB(u, STemp1)$;
$\qquad STemp = STemp1 \cup STemp$;
$\quad$ **end**
$\quad$ **if** ($MBTemp > MB$) **then**
$\qquad MB = MBTemp$;
$\qquad S = STemp$;
$\quad$ **endif**
endif
end
return MB;

Figure 10.1
Algorithm finding selection that maximizes replacement benefit

Algorithm $Feasible(R)$ is called which uses $O(|E_v|+|V_v|)$ time, by Thm. 9.4. So the time spent on node v is $O((|E_v|+|V_v|) \times 2^{|R_v|})$. Adding up for all the nodes in T, we have

$$O\left(\sum_{v \text{ in } T} \left((|E_v|+|V_v|) \times 2^{|R_v|}\right) \right). \quad \blacksquare$$

To get a feeling about the time complexity of the bound in the proof of Thm. 10.2, note that R_v are empty for most of the v's. Even when R_v is not empty, it will be extremely small (perhaps containing one or two replacements) in practice.

10.4   Evaluation of Savings

To evaluate the value of $savings(r)$ for a replacement r, we need to have performance information on the replacing library procedure and the statements to be replaced. The performance of the replacing library procedure can be evaluated off-line. It can be expressed as a function of some input parameters, typically those governing the loop iterations and truth value of conditional statements.

Although we cannot evaluate the statements until we find out what they are by pattern matching, we do have the pattern that they are supposed to match. Therefore, the performance of the statements can also be "evaluated" off-line, by evaluating off-line the pattern related to the library procedure. (Section 2.2 discusses the relationship between a pattern and a library procedure.) Again, the performance of the pattern can be expressed as a function of some input parameters. The actual values of these input parameters will be known after pattern matching. They are part of the constraints under which the statements match the pattern. The constraints are known by the time we need to use the value for $savings(r)$ for replacement selection. Therefore, we can pre-evaluate $savings(r)$, expressing it as a function of some input parameters.

The savings realized are dependent upon the target architecture. For example, for a uniprocessor system, rough performance estimates can be based on counting floating point operations and memory operations, weighted by their respective **latencies**.

For a multi-processor shared-memory system, rough performance estimates begin with counting floating point operations and memory operations, weighted by their respective latencies. These values must be separated into those that occur in sequential and parallel sections of the program. The counts for the parallel sections may be divided by the number of processors that are expected to be applied, scaled by a factor that accounts for parallel execution overhead. If **synchronization** operations are performed, their latencies also must be included.

For a multi-processor distributed-memory system, rough performance estimates need to comprehend the time taken to send and receive messages, in addition to the basic floating point and memory operation counts. Sophisticated models for evaluating the performance of parallel programs are beyond the scope of this work.

10.5   Summary

- The performance of a potential procedure for replacement can be evaluated offline, as can the performance of the statements being replaced.
- The parameters of a savings function include the number of iterations of a loop and the truth value of conditional statements.
- The savings derived from a replacement depend on the target architecture.

11 Performing Algorithm Replacements

This chapter discusses how to carry out a feasible set of algorithm replacements to the computational kernel. We first present the details for replacement with library procedure calls. We then discuss the alternatives to such replacements.

11.1 Replacement with Library Procedure Calls

An algorithm replacement replaces one or more statements of the computational kernel executed under the same control flow with a semantically equivalent library procedure call. We perform algorithm replacements on the control tree T representing the computational kernel. If multiple statements are to be replaced by one procedure call, these statements must be children of the same control-group node.

Replacements performed inside different subtrees do not interfere with each other. They can be carried out independently. It is relatively simple to replace a single statement that is not a child of a control-group node in T.

Performing several replacements each involving multiple children statements of the same control-group node is more complex. Our approach is to find a valid statement ordering for the children statements of the control-group node, such that statements in the same algorithm replacement are listed together. Since the set of replacements to be performed on T is feasible, such a valid statement ordering does exist. The replacements are performed on T in a bottom up fashion. The details are given in Fig. 11.1.

For implementation purposes, the members of S are scattered throughout T. In particular, if $r \in S$ is to replace some children statements of node v in T, then r is attached to v.

Figure 5.15 contains the basic construct representing a procedure call. Such a basic construct is stored with each algorithm pattern. The actual parameters for the call have been decided as constraints during algorithm pattern matching. The computational kernel and the replacing library procedure may be coded in different programming languages having different parameter passing conventions, such as pass-by-value or pass-by-reference. Special care must be taken before the constraints from pattern matching can be used as actual parameters for the call. Details will be discussed in Sect. 11.1.

THEOREM 11.1: The time complexity of Algorithm

$PerformAlgorithmReplacements()$ is $O(|T| + \sum_{i=1}^{m}(|E_i| + |V_i|))$ time, where T stands

---

Procedure *Perf ormAlgorithmReplacements*(*T*, *S*)
Input:

1. *T*: the control tree representing the computational kernel. For each control-group node *v* in *T*, there is a statement-level data flow dependence graph *G* for the children of *v*.
2. *S*: the best selection of algorithm replacements (on *T*), computed by Function *MB*() (refer to Sect. 10.3)

Output:

1. *T*: the control tree representing the computational kernel. *T* is modified due to algorithm replacements. It still represents a program which is semantically equivalent to the original computational kernel.

Process:

Traverse *T* in post-order, do the following upon visiting a node *v*:

if (there is $r \in S$ to be performed on *v*'s children) **then**

    if (*v* is not a control-group node) **then**

        Let *u* be one of *v*'s children, and $r \in S$ be the algorithm replacement to performed at *u*. (*u* is not a control-group node either. A replacement never occurs at a control-group node.)

        Replace *u* as a child of *v* with a special new node, which is the root of the subtree representing the (library) procedure call introduced by algorithm replacement *r*.

    else

        Let *G* be the statement-level data flow dependence graph. Let $r_1, r_2, ..., r_k$ be members in *S* that need to be performed on *v*'s children. Let $s_1, s_2, ..., s_q$ be the strongly connected components of *G* which are disjoint with all of $r_1, r_2, ..., r_k$.
As discussed in Sect. 8.1, any strongly connected component is either disjoint with or a subset of r_i $(1 \leq i \leq k)$.

        In graph *G*, collapse each r_i $(1 \leq i \leq k)$ into a special node, which is the root of the subtree representing the procedure call introduced by algorithm replacement r_i. Let G_1 be collapsed graph.

        In graph G_1, collapse each s_j $(1 \leq j \leq q)$ into a special node α_i. Let G_2 be resultant directed acyclic graph.

        Topologically sort the vertices of G_2, giving the topological sequence *L*.

        Replace each α_i $(1 \leq i \leq q)$ in *L* with vertices of strongly connected component s_i, listing the vertices of s_i according to their original relative order in the source program. Let $v'_1, v'_2, ..., v'_m$ be the resultant sequence after all such replacements.

        In *T*, update *v*'s children list by making $v'_1, v'_2, ..., v'_m$ the only children of *v*. G_1 is now the data flow dependence graph for $v'_1, v'_2, ..., v'_m$.

    endif

  endif

Figure 11.1
Algorithm to perform algorithm replacements

for the input control tree, and $G_i = (V_i, E_i)$ $(i = 1, ..., m)$ are the statement-level data flow dependence graphs in *T* before algorithm replacements are performed.

Proof. Traversing T takes at least $O(|T|)$ time. Consider the time spent on each node v. If no algorithm replacement takes place at v's children, or if v is not a control-group node, then only $O(1)$ time is required. Otherwise, it is necessary to do vertex collapsing and topological sorting of the statement-level data flow dependence graph on v's children. Vertex collapsing and topological sorting in a graph $G_i = (V_i, E_i)$ can be done in linear time $O(|E_i| + |V_i|)$. Adding up for all the nodes in T, the total time complexity of the algorithm is as claimed in the theorem. ∎

Actual Parameters for the Replacing Procedure Calls

Let st_1, st_2, ..., st_l be the statements to be replaced by the same library procedure call. During algorithm recognition, these statements were extracted from the computational kernel to form an extracted subprogram in order to compare with the algorithm patterns. For convenience, we will refer to this extracted subprogram as $I(y_1, y_2, ..., y_t)$, where y_j ($j = 1, ..., t$) are the variables in the statements. Let $P(x_1, ..., x_s)$ be the pattern that $I(y_1, y_2, ..., y_t)$ matches under the constraints $x_i = f_i(y_1, y_2, ..., y_t)$ ($i = 1, 2, ..., s$). We know that subprogram $P(f_1(y_1, ..., y_t), ..., f_s(y_1, y_2, ..., y_t))$ and $I(y_1, y_2, ..., y_t)$ are semantically equivalent. Let $PP(x_1, ..., x_s)$ be the library procedure corresponding to pattern $P(x_1, ..., x_s)$. If the computational kernel and the library are written both in Fortran or both in the C language, then we can replace the statements with a call $PP(f_1(y_1, ..., y_t), ..., f_s(y_1, y_2, ..., y_t))$.

Constructing the actual parameters of the library call can be complicated if the computational kernel and library are written in different programming languages. Different languages use different mechanisms for passing parameters. Fortran uses the pass-by-reference mechanism. C uses pass-by-value. A simple solution is to maintain separate libraries of replacing procedures for distinct languages that use different parameter passing conventions.

For example, consider the computational kernel of Fortran show in the upper subprogram in Fig. 11.2. As show in the lower subprogram, the code can be replaced by a call to a library procedure $prefixSum(x, y, n)$ that computes $x[j] = \sum_{i=1}^{j} y[i]$ (for $j = 1, ..., n$).

The control tree before and after algorithm replacement is shown in Fig. 11.3.

11.2 Alternatives to Library Calls

We have defined (in Chap. 9 and this chapter) the algorithm replacement problem to result in inserting a library procedure call. In this section we discuss alternatives to such replacement. Even in a system that implements one or more of these alternatives, however,

```
......
integer i,m,k
real A(*), B(*)
......
A(1) = B(1)
do i = 2, m+k
  A(i) = A(i-1) + B(i)
enddo
......
```

```
......
integer i,m,k
real A(*), B(*)
......
call prefixSum(A,B,m+k)
......
```

Figure 11.2
Subprogram before and after replacement

it must still support the fundamental feature of replacement with a call. This is the only approach that is meaningful under all circumstances described below.

One of the alternatives to a library call can be performed immediately when an algorithm is recognized, without performing a call replacement. It is easier, however, to consider them all to occur after a call replacement. The alternatives are then performed at a later stage in the compilation process. The alternatives available depend on the type of software system architecture in which algorithm recognition and replacement are embedded.

Preprocessor System Architecture

SOURCE CODE DEFAULT

A preprocessor generates source code from source code. If the algorithm recognition and replacement system is part of a preprocessor, the default behavior would be to generate a library call in source code.

SOURCE CODE INLINING ALTERNATIVE

The alternative to generating a source code procedure call is to substitute inline the body of the source code from the library procedure.

This alternative is the logical choice when both of the following conditions are true.

• The source code of the library procedure is available to the compiler.

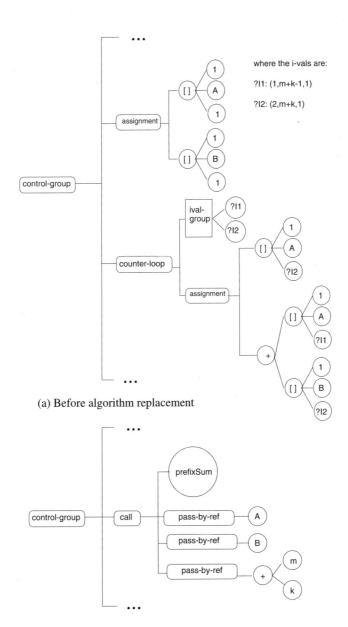

(a) Before algorithm replacement

(b) After algorithm replacement

Figure 11.3
The control tree before and after algorithm replacement

• The library procedure is written in the same high level language as that of the procedure being matched.

Integrated System Architecture

Object Code Default

If the algorithm recognition and replacement system is integrated into a compiler that generates object code, the default behavior would be to generate a standard library call during object code generation.

This approach is the logical choice when either of the following conditions are true.

• The replaced algorithm has a relatively large execution time, in comparison to the cost of a procedure call.

• The only version of the replacement algorithm is the object form of a library procedure.

Assembly Code Alternative

The first alternative is performed at the beginning of the code generation process. The library call can be replaced with a stream of assembly instructions that implement the library procedure. These instructions can have resources allocated to them and can be scheduled during code generation of the calling procedure. The code generator must tailor standard procedure call prologues and epilogues for passing arguments and returning results.

Under some circumstances, the specific assembly code that a human can write for a given algorithm may be far superior to what any general purpose compiler can generate. The specific assembly code may not be large enough to justify a procedure call, or achieving optimum performance of the calling procedure may require combined scheduling of several recognized algorithms. This approach is the logical choice when both of the following conditions are true.

• The replaced algorithm has a modest execution time.

• The assembly language source for the library procedure is available to the compiler.

Intermediate Code Alternative

The second alternative is performed immediately after algorithm recognition and replacement is finished. The library call can be replaced with the intermediate representation of the called procedure. This effectively substitutes inline the library procedure.

The benefit of this approach is that the library procedure is then subject to further analysis and optimization. This approach is the logical choice when all of the following conditions are true.

- The performance of the calling procedure or the entire application depends on further analysis of their respective parts.
- The library procedure was written in a high-level language.
- The intermediate representation for the library procedure is available to the compiler.

11.3 Summary

- Performing several replacements involving multiple children statements of the same control-group node requires finding a valid ordering of the children that places them contiguously.
- Constructing the call to a library procedure using the constraints of the match is straightforward when both the computational kernel and library procedure are written in the same language.
- Constructing a call to a library procedure is more complicated when the computational kernel and library procedure are written in different languages.
- Depending on the architecture of the system in which algorithm recognition and replacement is embedded, there are several alternatives to generating a call to a library procedure.

12 Time Complexity and Performance

The preprocessing transformations discussed in Chap. 4 are well known compiler optimizations. So we will focus on the analysis of the algorithm recognition and replacement phase. The time complexity of our approach is somewhat sensitive to the computational kernel being analyzed. The best way is to explain it is to show a flow chart and give the time complexity for each step of the chart.

12.1 Individual Step Complexity

The time complexities for the steps in Fig. 12.1 are given below.

In all steps, T refers to the control tree representing the whole computational kernel. T1 refers to the control tree for an extracted subprogram, and T2 refers to to the i-val tree for an extracted subprogram.

(a) and (b) in all iterations: $O\left(|T| + \sum_{\text{all } |V_v| \text{ in } T} 2^{|V_v|-1}\right)$ time in the worst case, where $|T|$ is the size of the control tree T representing the whole computational kernel, and each V_v represents set of children of a control-group node v in T. (Refer to Chap. 8, especially Thm. 8.2 and Sect. 8.3.)

(c) in one iteration: $O(\log L)$ time in the worst case, where L is the number of algorithm patterns in the database. (Refer to Sect. 7.4.)

(d) in one iteration: $O(1)$ time.

(e) in one iteration: The worst case time complexity is $O(|T1| \times log|T1|)$. (See Thm. 6.3.) In practice, the expected time complexity is $O(|T1|)$. (See Corollary 6.1.)

(f) in one iteration: $O(1)$ time.

(g) in one iteration: The worst case time complexity is $O(|T1|^2 \times (s + t))$, where $|T1|$ is the size of the control tree representing the extracted subprogram, s is the number of distinct variable names, and t is the number of distinct i-val references in $T1$. (See Thm. 6.4.)

(h) in one iteration: $O(|T1| + \sum_{i=1}^{m}(|E_i| + |V_i| \times \log |V_i|))$ time in the worst case, where $G_i = (V_i, E_i)$ $(i = 1, ..., m)$ are the the statement-level data flow dependence graphs in $T1$. (Refer to Thm. 6.5.)

(i) in one iteration: The worst case time complexity is $O(|T1| + |T2|)$. (Refer to Sect. 6.5.)

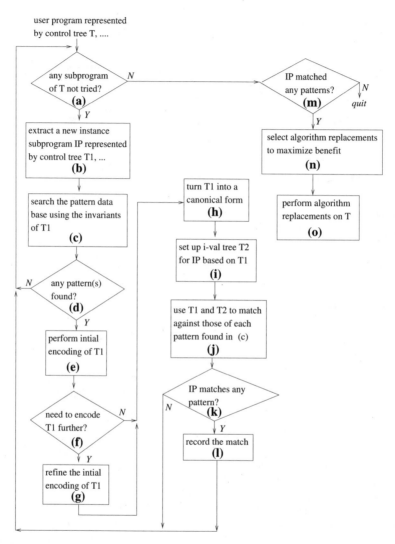

Figure 12.1
Algorithm recognition and replacement system flow chart

(j) in one iteration: Matching $T1$ against that of a pattern takes $O(|T1|)$ time in the worst case. (Refer to Thm. 7.1.) Matching $T2$ against that of a pattern takes $O(|T2| + m^2 * l)$ time in the worst case (refer to Thm. 7.2), where m is the number of i-vals of the pattern subprogram that contain free variables, and l is the number of free variables in the i-vals of the extracted subprogram.

In practice, both m and l tend to be extremely small relative to the size of the control tree T1, whose size is about the same as the size of subprogram IP represented partly by T1 (as discussed in Sect. 5.8). Therefore, we can expect step (j) to be done in $O(|T1| + |T2|) = O(|IP|)$ time, where $|IP|$ is the number of lexical tokens in IP.

(k) in one iteration: $O(1)$ time.

(l) in one iteration: $O(1)$ time.

(m) in one iteration: $O(1)$ time.

(n) The worst case time complexity is $O\left(\sum_{v \text{ in } T} \left((|E_v| + |V_v|) \times 2^{|R_v|}\right)\right)$, where T is the control tree representing the whole computational kernel being optimized. (E_v, V_v) represents the statement-level data flow dependence graph on the children statements of node v in T. R_v represents the set of algorithm replacements (matches found) on the children of v. (Refer to Thm. 10.2.) In practice, R_v is expected to be empty for most of v's. Even if it is not empty, R_v will probably contain an extremely small number of elements (algorithm replacements).

(o) The worst case time complexity is $O(|T| + \sum_{i=1}^{m}(|E_i| + |V_i|))$, where $G_i = (V_i, E_i)$ $(i = 1, ..., m)$ are the the statement-level data flow dependence graphs in T before algorithm replacements are performed (Thm. 11.1).

12.2   Total Algorithm Complexity

In summary, the recognition and replacement phase has one big loop (a)–(l), and several steps (m)–(o) outside the loop. Steps (m)–(o) are less expensive than the loop. In each loop iteration, a subprogram IP is extracted from the computational kernel and processed. The total number of iterations of the loop is exactly as many as the number of extracted subprograms that are computationally confluent. In the worst case, it is bounded

by $O\left(|T| + \sum_{\text{all } |V_v| \text{ in } T} 2^{|V_v|-1}\right)$ where T is the control tree representing the whole computational kernel. Each V_v is the set of children of a control-group node v in T. (These children are statements executed under the same control flow.) In practice, the worst case rarely happens (see Sect. 8.3), and the $|V_i|$'s tend to be very small.

For each iteration involves steps to match IP against the patterns in the database, with the time complexity being the following.

- At most $O(\log L)$ time is needed if early loop exit is taken at (d), where L is the number of patterns in the database. This is expected to be most of the cases in practice.
- If no early loop exit is taken, the most expensive step is (g). This is not expected to be necessary for most cases in practice. The second most expensive steps are (e) and (h). All other steps need no more than $O(|IP|)$ expected time.

12.3   Complexity and Heuristics

Our subprogram extraction heuristic is based on the concept of Computational Confluence, which describes the properties of a set of statements under the same control flow. In our internal representation, given a Control-Group node v with k children (statements), there can be in the worst case 2^k sets of the statements that are Computationally Confluent. Therefore, our extraction algorithm, though optimal, takes $O(2^k)$ time in the worst case to extract all the subprograms under the Control-Group node. However, we believe that this worst case bound is seldom reached. It would require the statement level data flow dependence graph (for children of v) to have a very special topology. Even if this worst case bound is reached, note that k, the number of children of v (or the statements under the same control flow) tends to be a small number in practice.

See App. D for experimental data that support this assertion.

13 Conclusion

13.1 Our Contributions

We establish a fundamentally new theoretical framework for automatic algorithm recognition and replacement.

There are basic differences between our approach to algorithm recognition and previous work on the "program understanding problem". In previous work, program understanding is defined as determining whether a section of code can be generated by grammar rules in a database. In some works, this definition is explicit, in others implicit. The representations of a code section include source text, syntax trees, graphs, etc.

This definition leads to rule-based implementation methods. Heuristics are usually included to improve the execution speed of these methods. These heuristics focus on organizing and retrieving the rules in the database.

In our approach, algorithm pattern matching is defined as the process of determining whether a relation exists between two syntactically valid sections of code. The representation of a code section is immaterial to the definition. Our heuristics focus on speeding up the comparison of these code sections.

This framework leads to the first algorithmic method for solving the algorithm recognition problem. Within this framework, it becomes both possible and easy, for the first time, to quantify and compare the efficiencies of different solutions as well as the quality of their outputs. It also enables us to obtain a complete solution for both the recognition and replacement problems.

We have addressed all of the technical issues identified in Sect. 1.4:

Extent: Will semantic analysis and optimization be performed on expressions, statements, statement groups, loop nests, procedures, or even entire programs?

Ordering: Will different orderings of operands or program statements be recognized as equivalent when they are in fact equivalent?

Variation: Will different choices of programming language constructs be recognized as equivalent when they achieve the same purpose?

Focus: Will there be a mechanism to focus the semantic analysis on program elements that are more important?

Non-Contiguousness: Will the relationship between logically related program elements that were not lexically adjacent be recognized?

Selection: If multiple optimizations are indicated as a result of program analysis, how will the best optimizations be chosen?

Correctness: If the resulting semantic analysis is used to guide optimization, how can the correctness of the transformations be ensured?

Scalability: Will the proposed methods scale to work on real applications (100,000 or more source lines) with a knowledge database large enough (1,000 or more algorithms) to recognize most realizations of the major techniques in use today?

We have fully solved each of these problems, except the two that have heuristic solutions.

Our contributions can be organized into the areas of algorithm recognition, algorithm replacement, implementation efficiency, and ease of use.

Algorithm Recognition

• We give a formal and exact definition of the general problem of algorithm pattern matching in terms of algorithmic instance testing. We also present results concerning their computational complexities. See Chap. 2.

• We provide a detailed taxonomy of the sources of program variation. It is correlated with the semantics-preserving transformations that compilers can perform to minimize the variation. See Chap. 4. We propose using a powerful interprocedural compiler to perform preprocessing of computational kernels prior to attempting algorithm pattern matching. This addresses the technical issue of variation.

• We identify the necessity of matching type expressions as well as computational expressions in order for replacements to be valid. We provide a solution within the context of our approach. See Sect. 7.1. This addresses one aspect of the technical issue of correctness.

• We define a new set of criteria for identifying portions of a program that are functionally related. See Chap. 8. Previous work on program understanding (25) (33) has only used **program slicing** (50) to achieve this purpose. We found slicing to be unusable when replacing statements. Depending on how it is applied, slicing either selects isolated nodes in a tree or graph, which cannot be replaced, or it selects almost every part, which is useless. This addresses an aspect of the technical issue of non-contiguousness.

• We describe the architecture of a system that performs full interprocedural analysis as a preprocessing system. This addresses the technical issue of extent.

Algorithm Replacement

• We raise the issue of conflicts that can occur when variables are renamed, unless consistency constraints are maintained across the whole procedure. See Sect. 7.3. This addresses another aspect of the technical issue of correctness.

• We find a necessary and sufficient condition for the feasibility of a set of statement replacements. See Sect. 9.2. This condition is expressed in terms of the topological properties of the data flow dependence graph. Thus, we have a linear time algorithm to test the condition. This addresses another aspect of the technical issue of correctness.

• We apply dynamic programming to solve the problem of selecting the best set of algorithm replacements. See Chap. 10. This addresses the technical issue of selection.

Implementation Efficiency

• We identify the necessity of using profile information to guide algorithm recognition when processing real applications. We use this information to create a representation of the core of the application. See Sect. 2.1 and A.1. This addresses the technical issue of focus.

• We handle alternative ordering by putting the internal representation into a canonical order. This uses a special tree sorting scheme. All previous work has either used exhaustive enumeration or has not addressed the issue. This addresses the technical issue of ordering.

• We propose a new method of matching pattern programs and extracted subprograms. It does not involve graph parsing or non-deterministic *if-then* rule evaluation. See Chap. 7.

• We define a representation for patterns that makes it possible to use integers to index them by simple graph invariants. This makes it possible to speed up the recognition process with a logarithmic time search of an index for the pattern database. Patterns from the database are not retrieved unless their index entries match the invariant values of the code being compared. See Sect. 7.4. This addresses an aspect of the technical issue of scalability.

Implementation Ease of Use

• We define a pattern representation such that a new algorithm pattern and its replacement can be easily added by a programmer. This person does not need to know how the system operates internally. All that is required is a source program defining the pattern and the name of the replacing library procedure. Previous approaches require the implementor of the system to derive new graph grammar rules or *if-then* rules, as well as constraints typically written in the implementation language. See Chap. 5.

In addition to fully addressing all of the technical issues we have raised, our work includes some new algorithmic techniques that are of interest in their own right. We present the new algorithmic techniques for tree orientation and tree encoding, used in tree sorting. See Chap. 6. We present an optimal algorithm to compute connected components in an undirected graph. See Sect. 8.2.

13.2   Future Research

Type Expressions

In Sect. 5.3, we described our approach to representing type expressions. Our current approach to types allows limited use of pointers. Pointers and arrays are both resolved to the *vector* type constructor. We do not provide a type constructor for non-homogeneous types, such as *struct* in C.

We made this choice because non-homogeneous types do not occur in most existing scientific applications. Thus our approach is sufficient for many applications we wish to analyze.

There are two trends in scientific computation that make us want to extend our design. First, changes in numerical methods are resulting in increased use of data structures that require either vectors of indices or pointers for indirection. The pointer approach results in non-homogeneous data types. Second, C++ is being used more in scientific applications. The fundamental construct in C++ is the non-homogeneous *class* type.

In the future, we would like to find a way to represent and analyze non-homogeneous data types in our approach.

Partial Matches

The approach described in this book was developed to accommodate a large amount of variation in programming and still be able to recognize and replace subprograms that are algorithmic instances of each other. There are times, however, when it would be desirable to be able to recognize subprograms that are similar in some sense, but are not algorithmic instances.

There are at least two places in our approach where we could look for partial matches. We can treat the set of invariants for a given tree as a vector in N-space. If there is no exact match of the invariants of an instance subprogram with any pattern subprogram in the pattern database, we could then optionally look for the "most similar" subprogram. A natural definition of similarity is to look for the invariant vector in the database that has the smallest difference in length, and the smallest difference in the angle formed by the two vectors.

The depth-first comparison of oriented trees offers another opportunity to identify "similar" subprograms. If an exact match didn't occur, a second depth-first search could compare nodes based on equivalence classes, rather than require an exact match. For example, all binary arithmetic operators could be considered as matching for similarity. All numeric constants could be another equivalence class, all scalar variables could be another equivalence class, and so on.

In the future, we would like to explore the concept of algorithm similarity and implement approaches for identifying similar algorithms.

Stylistic Considerations

Compilers that performed automatic vectorization were maturing during the first half of the 1980's. At that time, users of these compilers began to recognize that there was a "vector-friendly" style for writing scientific applications. Using this style minimized the problems such compilers would have vectorizing the code.

It is likely that as compilers that perform automatic algorithm recognition and replacement mature, users of these compilers will recognize stylistic considerations that make it easier for the compiler to perform this analysis.

In the future, we would like to frame the limits of automatic algorithm recognition and replacement in terms of programming style.

13.3   Other Applications of Our Work

The techniques developed in this book can be applied to several other uses beyond the original intent of program optimization. Three areas of application are obvious: software re-engineering of existing applications, programming instruction, and computer science research.

Software Engineering

There are several ways that our algorithm recognition techniques can be used to proactively improve desirable qualities of software.

As we noted earlier, "homegrown" scientific applications often do not make use of numerical libraries. In addition, the developers of these applications often use naive implementations of algorithms found in numerical analysis texts. Even when the implementation is well done, it is sometimes a poor choice to solve a given problem. For example, users who need to solve a system of linear equations are normally better served by an LU Decomposition algorithm than by using Gaussian Elimination.

Due to the numerical character of some algorithms, it is not always possible to replace one algorithm with another automatically. It is inappropriate for an optimizing compiler to do this if there is not a guaranteed speedup. But it is quite appropriate for a software re-engineering tool to identify the use of one algorithm and suggest the use of another, without actually performing the replacement, if the alternative gives a speedup for many possible input sets.

A second area in which algorithm recognition can be used to improve software is in the detection of fragile implementations of standard algorithms. Often programmers implement the algorithms they find in a book, without doing all the checks that might be useful and necessary. For example, when solving systems of linear equations, it is wise to perform various checks for singularities. If the implementation never processes an invalid input of this sort, the checks will not be missed.

It is not appropriate for an optimizing compiler to replace an algorithm with another that performs more checks than the original, since there will not be mechanisms to receive and handle various error return codes. But it is quite appropriate for a software re-engineering tool to recognize fragile implementations of common algorithms and recommend replacing them with a more robust version.

A third area in which algorithm recognition can be used to improve software is in the detection of computations that have undesirable numerical qualities. A good simple example is the catastrophic cancellation caused when summing a sequence of positive and negative floating point numbers whose magnitude is significantly different from the result. The problem code could be recognized and replaced with a version that sorts the values before summation.

Programming Instruction

A second area that our techniques could be applied is in assisting those who are teaching or learning programming languages. To assist the teacher, our approach could be used to perform automatic grading of programming assignments. Correct implementations can be recognized, and even partially correct implementations with common errors. This grading recognition can be used to supplement black-box testing of student programs.

To assist the student, the algorithm database could be populated with incorrect implementations of algorithms they are implementing. If the student has a problem, he can submit his program to the algorithm recognizer. If it recognizes his faulty algorithm, it can provide an appropriate diagnosis of the problem.

Computer Science Research

The final area that our techniques could be applied to takes a somewhat different approach than the first two. In those, our techniques were applied to applications using specialized databases of algorithms. In this third area, the point is to start with an empty database and automatically create it.

The idea here is to run part of the algorithm recognition tool over a large base of applications that are of interest to the researcher. The subprograms are extracted from the computational kernels of the application, and stored in the database. Matching is not performed. The key here is that we have a means of extracting all of the interesting computations that can in some sense stand alone. Our concept of computational confluence enables us to identify all of these code segments, which may be overlapping and hierarchically composed.

This database would then be used to improve the focus and quality of numerical libraries, compiler optimizations, and hardware architectures. Today, researchers and product developers working in these areas are dependent on synthetic benchmarks, or extracts from applications. The former will run quickly on a hardware simulator, but don't necessarily reflect the real workload a new processor will handle. The latter do reflect real workloads, but can take too long to run to be of use.

Rather than rely on the subjective opinions of people who construct synthetic benchmarks, this database would enable researchers and product developers to focus on making the code segments that really matter in real applications run faster. They could do this by implementing new library functions, inventing new compiler optimizations, or designing new hardware features that address these codes. Subprogram extraction by computational confluence can find all of the interesting computations, and researchers can select those that fit their simulation budgets.

13.4   Final Thoughts

For over a half-century, programmers have sought tools that enabled them to write at ever-higher levels of abstraction. There was a time when "automatic programming" meant the translation of assembly code into binary code. Today's programmer would expect far more from tool that claimed to perform "automatic programming".

In a similar way, programmers have ever-increasing expectations of the performance of optimizing compilers. With the first Fortran compiler, the question was whether the generated code could compete with hand-written assembly code. Today, optimizing compilers are expected to deal with languages that are harder to optimize, such as C++ and Java. We believe that in the coming decade, programmers will demand yet more performance from the compilers they use, and that automatic algorithm recognition will be one technology that makes satisfying this demand possible.

A Appendix: System Architecture

This appendix presents the high-level design for a software system that implements the ideas presented in this book. The detailed module design is found in App. B.

A.1 System Structure

In Chap. 4, we presented a catalog of sources of program variation and compiler transformations that can be used to minimize their effects. In our approach, we will use an existing compiler that already contains most of these transformations to preprocess computational kernels. The compiler, called the Application Compiler (34) (36), provided loop-level, procedural, and interprocedural optimizations. This compiler was a product offered by Convex Computer Corporation, now a part of the Hewlett-Packard Company.

Figure A.1 shows our proposed system architecture. First, the driver invokes a special version of the Application Compiler driver to handle preprocessing the source. This executable is called **arpa**. Then the driver invokes a program that can extract selected information from the Program Database generated by the Application Compiler. It uses information from an execution profile to determine which procedures to investigate. This executable is called **browser**. Finally, the driver executes the algorithm recognition and replacement sub-system.

The Application Compiler

The Application Compiler processes programs containing FORTRAN and C source code. The driver program for the Application Compiler determines which source files need to be compiled, and applies the appropriate front end to those files. The front end performs lexical analysis, syntactic analysis, and semantic analysis. It writes to disk the symbol table, annotated parse tree, and miscellaneous information for each procedure. These executables are called **ffront** and **cfront**.

After all source files that need to be (re)compiled have been processed, the driver invokes the first phase of the interprocedural optimizer. This executable is called **synth1** (synthesis phase 1). The first phase resolves the question of name association. Each analysis algorithm reads from the program database, and writes the information it generates back to that database. The following analyses are performed in the order listed.

- Interprocedural Type Checking – Which calls have type clashes and which globals are declared incompatibly in different source files?
- Interprocedural Call Analysis – Which procedures are invoked by each call?

- Interprocedural Alias Analysis – Which names refer to the same location?
- Interprocedural Pointer Tracking – Which pointers point to which locations?

After the first phase of interprocedural optimization, the driver runs a special version of the scalar optimizer. It has been modified to make use of information gathered in resolving names. It uses call targets and aliases that are exact (for Fortran) or much more constrained (for C). This executable is called **mend** (middle end).

The second phase of interprocedural optimization resolves the question of side effects. It also performs true interprocedural optimizations. This executable is called **synth2** (synthesis phase 2). Each analysis algorithm reads from the program database, and writes the information it generates back to that database. The following analyses are performed in the order listed.

- Interprocedural Scalar Analysis – Which procedures (and subordinates) use and assign which scalars?

- Interprocedural Constant Propagation – Which globals and arguments are constant on entry to which procedures?

- Inline Analysis – Which procedures should be inlined at which call sites? Subroutines and functions are both candidates for inlining, though the optimizer does not attempt to inline procedures written in one language into a procedure written in another language.

- Clone Analysis – Which procedures should be duplicated so that they can be modified with information about a specific call site?

- Interprocedural Array Analysis – Which procedures (and subordinates) use and assign which sections of arrays?

- Storage Optimization – How should application data structures be rearranged to improve the usage of the memory hierarchy?

After the interprocedural algorithms have completed, the driver program invokes a special version of the compiler common back end for each procedure in the application. This optimizer has been modified to make use of information gathered by interprocedural analysis phase, rather than make worst-case assumptions about procedure side-effects. This executable is called **pend** (penultimate end).

The normal back end consists of a machine-independent optimizer and a machine-dependent code generator. In the version of the Application Compiler used for algorithm recognition and replacement, we only perform those optimizations and loop transformations that are useful for reducing program variation. In addition to omitting several optimizations and transformations, we also modified some for our special purposes, and added several new ones. Instead of a code generator, we substituted a module that generates the representation documented in App. C.

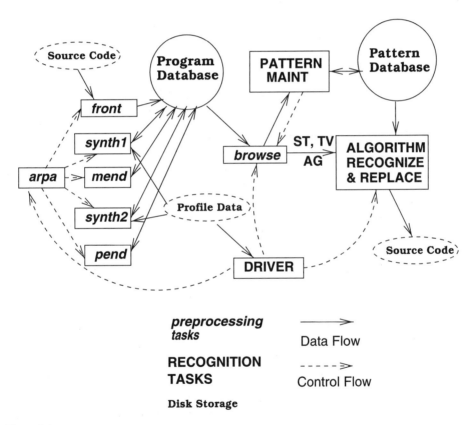

Figure A.1
Algorithm recognition and replacement system architecture

Selecting Computational Kernels

The Application Compiler can read information from an execution profile and store this in its program database. Providing a profile as an input is a requirement for our approach.

The driver selects from the database the representations of all computational kernels that use five percent or more of the total CPU time of the application. We chose this value empirically, based on a review of the profiles of a number of benchmarks and applications. The version of the Application Compiler we use has been modified to perform procedure call inlining on the same basis. Thus the procedures retrieved have had the entire dynamic call tree inlined into them.

A.2   Data Flow

Figure A.2 provides a more detailed data flow diagram of the system design. Following (13), it uses the following notation.

- Arcs with arrows represent data paths.
- Ellipses (bubbles) represent processes transforming data.
- Heavy lines represent databases.
- Boxes represent sources or sinks of data outside of the system.

The compiler performs transformations that reduce program variation, resulting in a control flow graph consisting of directed acyclic graphs representing basic blocks, along with symbol information. The final phase of the special preprocessing compiler generates an acyclic graph, a symbol table, and a type vector, as specified in App. C.

The algorithm recognition and replacement system will begin by generating the statement-level dependence graph, the i-val tree, and the control tree. The process of extracting a subprogram results in versions of these data structures for that subprogram. When the system attempts to match an extracted subprogram with a pattern, it reads these same data structures from the pattern library for the candidate pattern. If there is a match, a match descriptor is generated.

The match descriptor and the control tree of the extracted subprogram are the inputs to the process of analyzing the benefits of replacements. This process generates a selection descriptor. This descriptor, together with the control tree, is used to perform the replacement. The resulting revised control trees and i-val trees can be used to generate a new source program.

A.3   Summary

- A special version of the Application Compiler performs semantics-preserving transformations.

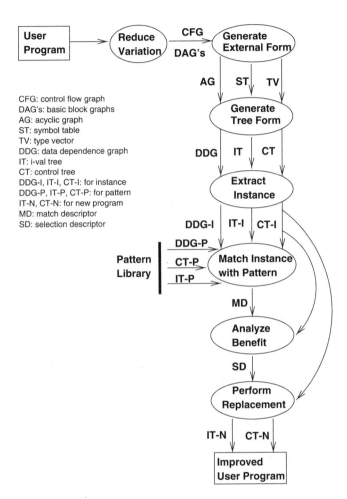

Figure A.2
Algorithm recognition prototype data flow

- Much of the work done by the system involves putting the program representation in a form best suited for the next task.

B Appendix: Module Design

This appendix detailed module design for software system that implements the algorithm recognition and replacement ideas presented in this book. The notation used in the figures shows procedures in boxes, connected to the procedures they invoke by arcs, with invocations embedded in loop annotated with a pointed ellipse.

B.1   Major Modules and Their Calling Relations

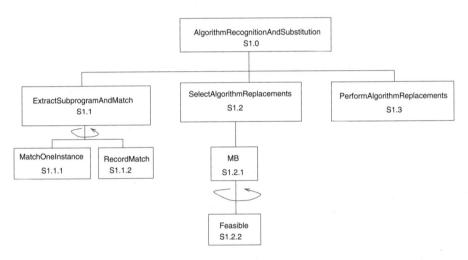

Figure B.1
Structure chart for algorithm recognition and replacement

s1.0: AlgorithmRecognitionAndSubstitution

s1.1: ExtractSubprogramsAndMatch()

comment: This module extracts "computationally confluent" groups of statements as extracted subprograms to match against the algorithm patterns. If a group of statements matches one of the algorithm patterns, this match is recorded at the statements' parent node in the control tree for the whole computational kernel.

input: • T: the control tree representing the computational kernel.

  • the statement-level data flow dependence graphs, one for each control-group. (Refer to Sect. 5.6.)

output: T in which each node v may be associated with a list $listOfMatches(v)$. In particular, each member r of $listOfMatches(v)$ records how a subset of v's children statements matches one of the algorithm patterns. So r is best implemented as a record containing at least the following information:

  • a subset of v's children

  • (pointer to) the algorithm pattern

  • the constraints under which the statements match the pattern

  • $saving(r)$. Because r can be seen as a potential algorithm replacement (as discussed in Chap. 10). $saving(r)$ will be used later for algorithm replacement selection.

s1.1.1: same as m1.0

s1.1.2: RecordMatch()

comment: When a match between v's children statements and one of the algorithm patterns is found, this module creates a new record and adds it to $listOfMatches(v)$. The record at least contains the following information:

  • a subset of v's children

  • (pointer to) the algorithm pattern

  • the constraints under which the statements match the pattern

  • $saving(r)$. Because r can be seen as a potential algorithm replacement (as discussed in Chap. 10). $saving(r)$ will be used later for algorithm replacement selection.

input: • T: the control tree representing the whole computational kernel.

  • v and the group of v's children statements matching one of the algorithm patterns.

  • the matched algorithm pattern

  • the constraints

output: $listOfMatches(v)$ updated

s1.2: SelectAlgorithmReplacements()

comment: After pattern matching, this module selects, among all the matches, a "feasible" set of algorithm replacements that maximizes the total benefits. Actually, it calls the recursive function "MB(root)" to do the job.

input: the output of s1.1

output: S: the "best" selection of algorithm replacements. (For implementation purpose, the members of S are scattered throughout the control tree T representing the whole computational kernel. In particular, if $r \in S$ is to replace some children statements of node v in T, then r is implemented as a subset of the children of v and r is attached to node v.)

s1.2.1: MB()

comment: Detailed algorithm under the same name can be found in Sect. 10.3.

s1.2.2: Feasible()

comment: Detailed algorithm under the same name can be found in Sect. 10.3.

s1.3: PerformAlgorithmReplacements()

comment: Detailed algorithm under the same name can be found in Sect. 11.1.

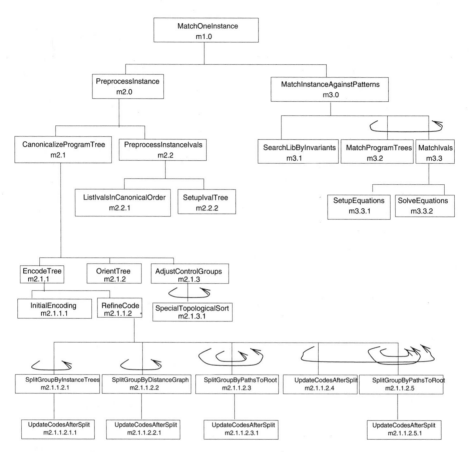

Figure B.2
Structure chart for matching an extracted subprogram against the patterns

m1.0: MatchOneInstance()

comment: Checks whether an extracted subprogram is an algorithmic instance of one the patterns in the database. If "yes", returns also the constraints for the match.

input: • *T*: the extracted subprogram control tree, not yet in the canonical form. (For example, see Fig. 5.24 on page 84.)

• the statement-level data flow dependence graphs, one for each control-group. (Refer to Sect. 5.6.)

• *ivalList*: the original list of i-vals along with their compiler generated identifications.

output: • "yes/no"

      • a pointer to the pattern (if "yes")

      • *constraints* (if "yes"). One possibility is to implement these using a global "table".

byproduct: T and the ivals will be represented in a canonical form

m2.0: PreprocessInstance()

comment: preprocess the extracted subprogram to get its representation (the extracted program control tree and the ivals) into a canonical form

input: • T: the extracted subprogram control tree (not yet in the canonical form),

      • $ivalList$: the original list of i-vals along with their compiler generated identifications.

      • the statement-level data flow dependence graphs, one for each control-group. (Refer to Sect. 5.6.)

output: • T: the extracted subprogram control tree in a canonical form

      • $ivalTree$: the i-val tree (read Sect. 6.5)

byproduct: • the i-vals will be given new identifications which are their positions in the canonicalized list of i-vals. (See Sect. 6.5.) (These new identifications will be compared between two corresponding i-val references when matching the extracted subprogram control tree and the pattern control tree, in Sect. 7.1 on page 117.)

m3.0: MatchInstanceAgainstPatterns()

comment: After preprocessing the extracted subprogram, match it against the patterns by comparing first the simple invariants, then the control trees and the i-val trees.

input: • T: the control tree of the extracted subprogram in a canonical form

      • $ivalTree$: the i-val tree of the (read Sect. 6.5)

output: • "yes/no"

      • a pointer to the pattern matched (if "yes")

      • *constraints* (if "yes")

m2.1: CanonicalizeControlTree()

comment: turns the control tree of the extracted subprogram into a canonical form

input: • T: the extracted subprogram control tree (not yet canonicalized),

      • $ivalList$: the original list of i-vals along with their compiler generated identifications.

- the statement-level data flow dependence graphs, one for each control-group. (Refer to Sect. 5.6.)

output: T: the extracted subprogram control tree in a canonical form.

m2.2: PreprocessInstanceIvals()

comment: list the i-vals in a canonical order and the i-vals will be given new identifications which are their positions in the canonicalized list of i-vals. (These new identifications will be compared between two corresponding i-val references when matching the extracted subprogram control tree and the pattern control tree, in Sect. 7.1 on page 117.) Also build the i-val tree. (read Sect. 6.5.)

input: • T: the extracted subprogram control tree in a canonical form.

             • $ivalList$: the original list of i-vals along with their compiler generated identifications.

output: • the canonicalized list of i-vals of the extracted subprogram.

             • the i-val tree of the extracted subprogram.

m3.1: SearchLibByInvariants()

comment: Use the simple invariants of the extracted subprogram to search the indexing structures of the pattern database. Return all the pointers to the patterns whose simple invariants match. (read Sect. 7.4.)

input: • invariants of the extracted subprogram.

             • the index of the pattern database.

output: a list of patterns whose simple invariants match.

m3.2: MatchControlTrees()

comment: Compare the extracted subprogram control tree with a pattern control tree. Both are in a canonical form. Detailed Algorithm is given in Sect. 7.1 on page 117.

m3.3: MatchIvals()

comment: Compare the i-vals of the extracted subprogram with the i-vals of a pattern. The idea is explained in Sect. 7.2.

input: • the i-val tree of the extracted subprogram

             • i-val tree of a pattern

             • pointer to the pattern (for other precomputed information about the pattern.)

output: • "yes/no"

             • $constraints$ updated to include the information from matching the i-vals.

m2.2.1: ListIvalsInCanonicalOrder()

comment: Read Sect. 6.5.

- T: the extracted subprogram control tree in a canonical form.
- $ivalList$: the original list of i-vals along with their compiler generated identifications.

output: the canonicalized list of i-vals of the extracted subprogram.

by product: the i-vals will be given new identifications which are their positions in the canonicalized list of i-vals. (read Sect. 6.5.) These new identifications will be compared between two corresponding i-val references when matching the extracted subprogram control tree and the pattern control tree. (details in Sect. 7.1 on page 117.)

m2.2.2: SetUpIvalTree()

comment: read Sect. 6.5 for details. Examples can be seen in Fig. 6.21, 7.4, and 7.5.

input:
- T: the extracted subprogram control tree in a canonical form.
- the output from "listIvalsInCanonicalOrder()"

output: the i-val tree of the extracted subprogram

m3.3.1: SetUpEquations()

comment: Comparing the extracted subprogram i-val tree with the pattern i-val tree node by node, and one equation is set up for each corresponding pair where the node of pattern tree represents a multilinear expression of free program variables. The detailed idea is given in Sect. 7.2.
To establish Eqn. 7.3 on page 121, we need the following matrices:

Precomputed: $A(m, n)$, and $D(m)$

Newly computed: $B(m, l)$, and $D'(m)$

m3.3.2: SolveEquations()

comment: solve the equations established by "setUpEquations()". The detailed idea is explained in Sect. 7.2
To solve equation Eqn. 7.3 on page 121, we need the following matrices:

Precomputed: $A'(m, m)$ and $W(m, n)$

Newly computed: $A'(m, m) \cdot B(m, l)$ and $A'(m, m) \cdot (D'(m) - D(m))$ (see Eqn. 7.5 on page 122)

Solution: can be expressed by Eqn. 7.7.

output: $constraints$: updated to reflect the solution.

m2.1.1: EncodeTree()

comment: This procedure merely contains two calls to "InitialEncoding()" and "RefineCode()".

input: same as "InitialEncoding()"

output: same as and "RefineCode()"

m2.1.2: OrientTree()

comment: details are given in an algorithm in Sect. 6.2.

m2.1.3: AdjustControlGroups()

comment: details are given in an algorithm in Sect. 6.4.

m2.1.1.1: InitialEncoding()

comment: details are given in an algorithm in Sect. 6.3.

m2.1.1.2: RefineCode()

comment: details are given in an algorithm in Sect. 6.3.

m2.1.1.2.1: SplitGroupByInstanceTrees()

    comment: details are given in an algorithm in Sect. 6.3. A demonstration is given in Fig(s). 6.10 and 6.11 on pages 103 and 104.

m2.1.1.2.2: SplitGroupByDistanceGraph()

    comment: details are given in an algorithm in Sect. 6.3. A demonstration is given in Fig(s). 6.13 and 6.14 on page 106 and 107.

m2.1.1.2.3: SplitGroupByPathsToRoot()

    comment: details are given in an algorithm in Sect. 6.3. A demonstration is given in Fig(s). 6.16 and 6.17 on page 109 and 110.

m2.1.1.2.4: UpdateCodesAfterSplit()

    comment: details are given in an algorithm in Sect. 6.3.

    input: • *code*: an array of records storing the distinct labels in the control tree and their current integer codes.

                • $G_1, ..., G_k$: the list of subgroups from splitting a larger group.

    output: *code*: updated to reflect the subgroups.

m2.1.1.2.5: similar to m2.1.1.2.3

m2.1.1.2.1.1: similar to m2.1.1.2.4

m2.1.1.2.2.1: similar to m2.1.1.2.4

m2.1.1.2.3.1: similar to m2.1.1.2.4

m2.1.1.2.5.1: similar to m2.1.1.2.4

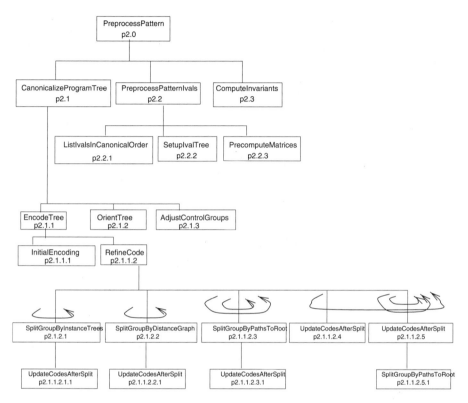

Figure B.3
Structure chart for preprocessing a pattern

p2.0: PreprocessPattern()

comment: preprocess the pattern to get its representation (the extracted subprogram control tree and the ivals) into a canonical form. Precompute some matrices used in the equation solver. (Read Sect. 7.4.)

input: • T: the pattern control tree (not yet canonicalized),

• $ivalList$: the original list of i-vals along with their compiler generated identifications.

• the statement-level data flow dependence graphs, one for each control-group. (Refer to Sect. 5.6.)

output: • T: the pattern control tree in a canonical form

• $ivalTree$: the i-val tree (read Sect. 6.5)

- $A(m, n)$, $A'(m, m)$, $D(m)$, and $W(m, n)$. (See Sect. 7.2 and 7.2.)

byproduct: • the i-vals will be given new identifications which are their positions in the canonicalized list of i-vals. (read Sect. 6.5.) (These new identifications will be compared between two corresponding i-val references when matching the extracted subprogram control tree and the pattern control tree, in Sect. 7.1 on page 117.)

p2.1*: similar to m2.1*

p2.2: PreprocessPatternIvals()

comment: list the i-vals in a canonical order and the i-vals will be given new identifications which are their positions in the canonicalized list of i-vals. Also build the i-val tree. (read Sect. 6.5.) (These new identifications will be compared between two corresponding i-val references when matching the extracted subprogram control tree and the pattern control tree, in Sect. 7.1 on page 117.)

input: • T: the pattern control tree in a canonical form.

   • $ivalList$: the list of i-vals along with their compiler generated identifications.

output: • the canonicalized list of i-vals of the extracted subprogram.

   • $ivalTree$: the i-val tree of the pattern.

   • $A(m, n)$, $A'(m, m)$, $D(m)$, and $W(m, n)$

p2.3: similar to m2.3

p2.2.1: similar to m2.2.1

p2.2.2: similar to m2.2.2

p2.2.3: PrecomputeMatrices()

comment: Precompute some matrices based on the pattern control tree. These matrices will be used in equation solver. (To understand the idea, read Sect. 7.2 and 7.2.)

input: $ivalTree$: the i-val tree (read Sect. 6.5)

output: $A(m, n)$, $A'(m, m)$, $D(m)$, and $W(m, n)$

B.2   Major Data Structures

- control trees (See Fig. 5.24 on page 84.) The commutative, non-commutative, and semi-commutative operators are listed close to the beginning of Chap. 6.

- the statement-level data flow dependence graphs, one for each control-group. (Refer to Sect. 5.6.)

- The original list of i-vals with compiler generated identifications.

- The canonicalized list of i-vals with new identifications which are their relation position in the list. (These new identifications will be compared between two corresponding i-val references when matching the extracted subprogram control tree and the pattern control tree, in Sect. 7.1 on page 117.)

- i-val tree. (See Fig. 6.21, 7.4, and 7.5 on pages 116, 120, and 120.)

- *constraints*: this may be implemented as a table to keep track of the variable renaming and substitutions during matching. It needs to be updated after matching control trees and after matching i-vals. Don't forget consistency checking.

- The indexing structure of the database by simple invariants

- The matrices used in representing and solving the equations during i-val matching.

- Local data structures for encoding: (See Fig. 6.10 and 6.11 on pages 103 and 104, Fig. 6.13 and 6.14 on pages 106 and 107, Fig. 6.16 and 6.17 on pages 109 and 110.)

    –*code*: an array of records storing the distinct labels in the control tree and their current integer codes. This structure is used in the encoding scheme. See Fig. 6.10 and 6.11 on page 103 and 104.

    –A group of variables

    –A list of groups

    –A c-distance graph (matrix representation) (See Fig. 6.13 and 6.14 on pages 106) and 107)

    –A instance tree (See Fig. 6.10 and 6.11 on pages 103) and 104)

- Local data structures for the two algorithms in Sect. 6.4.

- $listOfMatches(v)$. v is a node in the control tree representing the whole computational kernel. Each member of $listOfMatches(v)$ is a record containing at the following information:

    –a subset of v's children

    –(pointer to) the algorithm pattern

    –the constraints under which the statements match the pattern

    –$saving(r)$. Because r can be seen as a potential algorithm replacement (as discussed in Chap. 10). $saving(r)$ will be used later for algorithm replacement selection.

- Local data structures for the algorithms in Sect. 8.1, 8.2, 10.3, and 11.1.

C Appendix: Input Definition

C.1 Introduction

This appendix presents the format of the input for a software system that implements the ideas presented in this book.

Each procedure analyzed by the algorithm recognition system is described by the following data structures:

- Symbol Table
- Type Vector
- Compute Graph

Thus this chapter contains three sections describing one of these data structures. The final section gives a complete listing of a procedure and the data structures that represent it.

Procedures to be analyzed by the algorithm recognition system are described by a symbol table, type vector, and compute graph. These data structures must be stored together as ASCII text in a file. The format of each data structure is a Scheme data object, either a list or a vector. Scheme lists are written in Cambridge Prefix form. Here is a list of four elements, the second of which is a list of three elements.

```
(a (b c d) e f)
```

Scheme vectors are written similarly, except they are prefixed by the character #. Here is a vector of four elements, the second of which is a list of three elements.

```
#(a (b c d) e f)
```

Further details on the syntax of Scheme can be found in: **Revised 4 Report on the Algorithmic Language Scheme.**

C.2 Symbol Table

The Symbol Table is stored in a Scheme vector. Each element of the vector is a list that defines one symbol. The list for one node has the structure of an "Alist" (association list). This means that each element of the Alist is itself a list of two items. The first item is a tag that is the means to access the second item.

Symbol Kinds

The first pair in a symbol Alist specifies the symbol kind. The following symbol kinds are used:

SK_ARRAY	array created by user
SK_ARRAY_TEMP	array created by compiler
SK_VARB	scalar created by user
SK_VARB_TEMP	scalar created by compiler
SK_PROGRAM	main program (Fortran only)
SK_BLOCK_DATA	block data procedure (Fortran only)
SK_SUBR	subroutine (Fortran only)
SK_FUNC	function
SK_INTRINSIC	runtime library procedure with no side-effects
SK_BUILTIN	runtime library procedure with side-effects
SK_EXTERNAL	name listed in EXTERNAL statement (Fortran only)
SK_COM_BLK	common block (Fortran only)
SK_EQUIV_GRP	equivalence group (Fortran only)
SK_NAMELIST	I/O namelist (Fortran only)
SK_TAG	a tag name (C only)
SK_TYPEDEF	a typedef entry (C only)

The value associated with the symbol kind is the symbol number for that symbol. The front ends generate symbol table entries for symbols that are not used in the optimizer. These symbols are not generated in the Symbol Table structure. As a result, there are symbol numbers that are not used.

The Application Compiler decomposes heterogeneous aggregate structures (C structures and unions) into simple arrays and scalars that have **pathref** names. For example, if the symbol table lexeme is "s.a.b.c", then the symbols listed are for "s", "a", "b", "c".

The Application Compiler converts a Fortran function or subroutine that has multiple entry points into multiple functions or subroutines that have single entry points. Thus we show no support for these language features in the symbol table.

Symbol Classes

Most symbols have a storage class. The following storage classes are used:

SC_STATIC	local static storage
SC_AUTO	local stack storage
SC_BASED	allocated offset from a base address
SC_ARG	argument
SC_ARG_PTR	address of an argument
SC_REG_ARG	register variable argument
SC_REG_ARG_PTR	address of a register variable argument
SC_REGISTER	register variable
SC_EXTDEF	external definition
SC_EXTREF	external reference
SC_MEMBER	member of an aggregate (union or structure)
SC_FUNC_RESULT	function result (Fortran)
SC_MEMORY	storage class for pointer targets / C arrays
SC_COMMON_VAR	Fortran common variable/array
SC_EQUIV_VAR	Fortran equivalenced variable/array
SC_DATA	initialized data
SC_TEXT	initialized read-only data

Symbol Attributes

Symbols can have a number of attributes. The following attributes are used:

SA_LEXEM	symbol name
SA_LINK_NAME	symbol name known by linker
SA_STORE_CLASS	symbol class (see above)
SA_TYPE_PREC	type and precision (see below)
SA_FLAGS	list of flags (see below)
SA_BLOCK	block number (C only)
SA_ARG_CNT	number of arguments (function or subroutine)
SA_DIMENSION	dimensionality of an array
SA_BOUNDS	bounds for each dimension of array
SA_OFFSET	byte offset of symbol within containing area
SA_SIZE	size in bytes of common block or equivalence group
SA_VALUE	value for a symbol (parameters, propagated constants)

SA_INIT_CNT	number of initializers in the initializer list
SA_INIT_LIST	values to initialize this name
SA_IPO_CONSTANT	value propagated to this name
SA_ARG_LIST	list of symbols of dummy arguments
SA_ALIASES	list of symbols that overlap storage for this symbol
SA_COM_BLK	common block symbol that contains this symbol
SA_COM_VARS	list of symbols in a common block
SA_EQUIV_GRP	equivalence group that contains this symbol
SA_EQUIV_VARS	list of symbols in an equivalence group
SA_NAMELIST	list of symbols in a namelist
SA_PATH_REF	list of symbols that compose this path reference
SA_RET_VAL	symbol containing return value of this function
SA_NEXT_NAME	link to next symbol of same name
SA_LAST_NAME	link to last symbol of same name

The attributes that refer to other symbols do so by referring to the symbol number, which is the index in the Symbol Table. These are: SA_DUMMY_ARGS, SA_ALIASES, SA_BOUNDS, SA_COM_BLK, SA_COM_VARS, SA_EQUIV_GRP, SA_EQUIV_VARS, SA_NAMELIST, SA_PATH_REF, SA_RET_VAL

The SA_NEXT_NAME and SA_LAST_NAME fields have indices into the vector that stores the symbol table.

Symbol Flags

The symbol flag attribute can have a number of tags. There are a large number of tags that might be used. The ones that might be useful in static analysis by an optimizer are listed below. The rest can be ignored.

SF_ARG_FLAG	symbol is a dummy argument
SF_FUNCTION_VALUE	stores results of a Fortran function
SF_EQUIV_TO_COMMON	put in common because equivalenced to a common variable
SF_USED_AS_ADJ_DIM	used as adjustable array dimension
SF_PASSED_BY_VALUE	used as actual argument passed by value
SF_PATH_REF	symbol is a pathref
SF_ALIAS_ADDR	aliasing occurs because address has been taken
SF_STAR_LENGTH	character variable length (*)
SF_CRAY_POINTER	a Cray-style pointer
SF_CRAY_POINTEE	a Cray-style pointee
SF_COMPILER_FORMAL	compiler created formal argument
SF_COMPILER_TEMP	compiler created temporary variable (char length specifiers)
SF_COMPILER_STRING	compiler created string variable
SF_AUTOMATIC_ARRAY	automatic array (Fortran 90)
SF_ALLOCATABLE_ARRAY	allocatable array (Fortran 90)
SF_TEMP_FOR_ADJ_DIM	temporary used to freeze adjustable array bounds

C.3   Type Vector

The Type Vector is stored in a Scheme vector. Each element of the vector is a list that defines one type. The list for one type contains two or three items. The first item in a type definition specifies the type constructor. The following type constructors are used:

Type Constructor

TC_BASE	base type
TC_ARRAY	array of prior type
TC_FUNC	function returning prior type
TC_PTR	pointer to prior type

If the first item was *not* TC_BASE, then the second item in a type definition is an index into the Type Vector that specifies the prior type the current type is constructed from.

Base Types

If the type constructor was TC_BASE, then the second item is a symbol that specifies the meaning of the base type. The following base types are supported:

TY_INTEGER*1	one byte signed integer
TY_LOGICAL*1	one byte logical (Fortran only)
TY_LOGICAL*2	two byte logical (Fortran only)
TY_LOGICAL*4	four byte logical (Fortran only)
TY_LOGICAL*8	eight byte logical (Fortran only)
TY_INTEGER*2	two byte signed integer
TY_INTEGER*4	four byte signed integer
TY_INTEGER*8	eight byte signed integer
TY_REAL*4	four byte floating point
TY_REAL*8	eight byte floating point
TY_REAL*16	sixteen byte floating point
TY_COMPLEX*8	eight byte complex floating point
TY_COMPLEX*16	sixteen byte complex floating point
TY_UNSIGNED*1	one byte unsigned integer (C only)
TY_UNSIGNED*2	one byte unsigned integer (C only)
TY_UNSIGNED*4	one byte unsigned integer (C only)
TY_UNSIGNED*8	eight byte unsigned integer (C only)
TY_CHAR	unsigned characters
TY_HOLLERITH	Hollerith characters (Fortran only)
TY_BITPATTERN	bit pattern (Fortran only)
TY_VOID	(C only)

If the third item exists, it provides additional information about the type construction. Its current purpose is to specify the bounds of array dimensions. It is a list of lists. Each item in the list is a pair, specifying the lower and upper bounds of one dimension.

C.4   Compute Graph

The Compute Graph is stored in a Scheme vector. Each element of the vector is a list that defines one node in the graph. The list for one node has the structure of an "Alist" (association list). This means that each element of the Alist is itself a list of two items. The first item is a tag that is the means to access the second item.

Node Kinds

The first pair in a node Alist specifies the node kind. The following node kinds are used:

NK_BLOCK   root node for basic block

Every basic block begins with one of these nodes. The initial block contains ASG nodes (without a value assigned) that root the start of reaching definition arcs for all scalar variables. The final block contains USE nodes that anchor the end reaching definition arcs for all scalar variables.

Constants and uses on the frontier of a basic block are connected to the BLOCK node of the basic block with a VD arc. BLOCK nodes are the targets of all branches.

NK_ASG   variable assignment

NK_USE   variable use

NK_ADDR   address of symbol

All three of these nodes can have input data flow arcs that serve to specify subscripts. The last input data flow arc of an ASG node specifies the source value to be stored. The ADDR node is like a USE node, except that it represents the address rather than the value of the named location.

NK_INTR   call intrinsic routine from runtime library

NK_BUILTIN   call builtin routine from runtime library

NK_CALLF   call user function

NK_CALLS   call user subroutine (Fortran only)

INTRINSIC nodes represent runtime library functions that return a result and have no side effects. BUILTIN nodes represent runtime library functions that have side effects. They may also return results. BUILTIN nodes can only modify their arguments.

NK_GOTO   one-way branch

NK_IF   two-way branch

NK_SELECT   multi-way branch

NK_RETURN   return from procedure

NK_REPEAT   exit node of loop preheader basic block

NK_END   exit node of loop postlatch basic block

NK_BREAK   exit from loop

NK_CONTINUE   next iteration of loop

Every basic block ends with one of these nodes. If one basic block simply follows another, the GOTO node is used. The IF node takes one input data flow arc which specifies the condition tested. The input must be an integer 0 or 1. The SELECT node takes one input data flow arc which specifies the branch to take, which must be an integer. The RETURN node takes one input data flow arc, which specifies the value to return from a function.

The IF, SELECT, and EXIT nodes all have the NA_BRANCH attribute, which specifies the possible branch targets and the values that select them. The first block of a loop contains an NK_REPEAT node, and the last block of the loop contains an NK_END node.

NK_CON   constant
NK_TEMP   temporary for by-reference passing of expressions
NK_PARENS   parenthesized expression (preserves order)
NK_IVAL   induction value sequence

The TEMP node is used to hold the values of expressions that are actual arguments to Fortran procedures. The PARENS node applies to any expression of numeric or character type.

The IVAL node requires three integer inputs. The first specifies the initial value of the integer sequence. The second specifies the final value. The third specifies the interval between values.

NK_NEG   negation
NK_ABS   absolute value
NK_ADD   add
NK_SUB   subtract
NK_MUL   multiply
NK_DIV   divide
NK_EXP   power

These arithmetic nodes apply to any numeric type. NEG and ABS take one input data flow arc. The others require two inputs.

NK_MAX   maximum
NK_MIN   minimum
NK_MOD   modulo

These arithmetic nodes apply to any integer or real type. They all require two inputs.

NK_EQ   equal
NK_GE   greater than or equal to
NK_GT   greater than
NK_LE   less than or equal to
NK_LT   less than
NK_NE   not equal
NK_UGE   unsigned greater than or equal to (C only)
NK_UGT   unsigned greater than (C only)
NK_ULE   unsigned less than or equal to (C only)
NK_ULT   unsigned less than (C only)

These relational nodes apply to any numeric type. They all require two inputs.

NK_NOT	not
NK_AND	and
NK_EQV	equivalent
NK_NEQV	not equivalent
NK_OR	or

These logical operators apply only to integer and logical types. NOT takes one input data flow arc. The others require two inputs.

NK_CONV	convert
NK_UCONV	unsigned convert
NK_SHIFT	shift (C only)

The CONV node converts the source data flow to the type of the CONV node. The UCONV node performs an unsigned conversion of the integer source to the integer type of the UCONV node. The SHIFT node requires two inputs. If the second is positive, the first input is shifted left, else it is shifted right. The magnitude of the first input specifies the number of bits to shift.

NK_STR_LEN	string length (Fortran only)
NK_STR_CONCAT	string concatenation (Fortran only)
NK_STR_CMP	string comparison (Fortran only)
NK_STR_ASG	substring assign (Fortran only)
NK_STR_USE	substring use (Fortran only)
NK_STR_ARG	substring argument (Fortran only)

These operators are used with Fortran CHARACTER type only.

NK_CNTL	common control environment

These are the only nodes that occur independently, outside of a basic block. A CNTL node has at least one output DF arc. The order of the targets of a CNTL node has no meaning. CNTL nodes are always the targets of IF nodes. All basic blocks that are the targets of the same CNTL node are always executed under the same control-flow conditions.

Node Attributes

Nodes can have a number of attributes. The following attributes are used:

NA_SOURCE	source line and column position of code originating this node
NA_SYMBOL	integer symbol number
NA_VALUE	integer, real, complex or character constant value
NA_TYPE_PREC	type and precision description (see TY_ labels above)

NA_FLAGS	node flags (see below)
NA_BRANCH	branch table (block exit nodes only)
NA_INTRINSIC	name of intrinsic (intrinsic nodes only)
NA_LOOP_LEVEL	integer loop nesting level (BLOCK nodes only)
NA_USES	list of symbol numbers possibly referenced (aliases/side-effects)
NA_ASGS	list of symbol numbers possibly assigned (aliases/side-effects)
NA_KILLS	list of symbol numbers definitely assigned (aliases/side-effects)
NA_BLOCK	basic block containing this node
NA_IN_DF	list of input data flow arcs
NA_IN_DD	list of input data dependence arcs
NA_OUT_DF	list of output data flow arcs
NA_OUT_DD	list of output data dependence arcs
NA_EXIT	exit branch node for this block
NA_NEXT_BLOCK	next block in block list
NA_LAST_BLOCK	last block in block list
NA_LOOP_HEAD	loop head of containing loop (BLOCK nodes only)
NA_LOOP_TAIL	last block of loop (BLOCK nodes only)

The branch table is a list of lists. Each list contains three elements. The first two are the low and high values, respectively, that select this branch target. The third value is the target BLOCK node. For IF nodes, the selection values are 1 (true) and 0 (false).

Arcs refer to other nodes by node number, which is simply the index of the node in the compute vector. Data flow (DF) arcs connect a node that produces a value with one that consumes it.

Data dependence arcs (DD) constrain the order in which nodes can be evaluated and retain the semantics of the original program. Each DD arc is defined by a list that contains the target node and a tag that defines the nature of the constraint. These arcs are built both for scalars and for arrays. The tags are defined as follows:

- F - a flow (true) dependence

- A - an anti dependence

- O - an output dependence

- I - an input dependence

All the arcs connecting nodes that define scalar variables (ASG, CALLF, CALLS,

BUILTIN) with those that use the values of those definitions (USE, CALLF, CALLS, BUILTIN) that are tagged F together form the set of reaching definitions.

The USES, ASGS, and KILLS attributes can appear on USE, ASG, CALLF, CALLS, and BUILTIN nodes.

There are several ways to traverse part or all of the compute graph. To visit every node in a basic block, begin with the block entry and sequentially process every node stored in the vector until you reach another block entry. The nodes of a basic block are stored in a topologically sorted order.

To visit every basic block, begin with the ENTRY node of the first block and follow the indices given in the NEXT_BLOCK field. Or begin with the EXIT node of the last block and follow the indices given in the LAST_BLOCK field. Blocks appear on the list in a topologically sorted order.

Node Flags

The node flag attribute can have a number of tags. There are a large number of tags that might be used. The ones that might be useful in static analysis prior to code generation are listed below. The rest can be ignored.

NF_COMP_GEN	compiler generated node (not source derived)
NF_COMP_GEN_SUB	compiler generated subscript
NF_COMPILER_ACTUAL	compiler generated actual argument
NF_RED_VARB	reduction variable
NF_CON_VARB	conditional induction variable
NF_NO_ASG_RECUR	assign is not a part of a recurrence
NF_PRE_PACKET	precompiled argument packet
NF_PASS_BY_REF	pass by reference (Fortran %REF)
NF_ADJ_ARRAY_TEMP	adjustable array temporary
NF_VOLATILE_ACCESS	C volatile variable

D Appendix: Statistics on Heuristic Behavior

D.1 Introduction

This appendix presents statistics that support some assertions about the behavior of some of our heuristics when handling real source code.

Indexing the Patterns by Simple Invariants

In Chap. 7, we asserted that by indexing our pattern database by a small number of graph invariants, we would be able to ensure that we could limit the comparison of any extracted subprogram to a very small number of patterns.

In this section, we present some statistics that show that for a basic database of patterns, using the representation that we propose in this book, the number of patterns that would be compared to any given subprogram is quite small.

We began to build our database of patterns by examining scientific applications and identifying the simplest loops nests that commonly occurred. When we found a common loop nest using a specific arithmetic operator, e.g. multiplication, we created versions of the loop nest that contained the same pattern of array and scalar references, but with each of the other scalar operators. This means that our initial database contains a number of sets of patterns which are the worst possible case for an indexing scheme based on graph invariants. The patterns in each set are identical, except for a single mathematical operator applied to the operands.

The initial database contains 536 patterns. The dyadic operators are: addition, subtraction, multiplication, division, exponentiation, modulo, low value, high value, logical and, logical or. The unary operators are: sum, product, maximum value, minimum value, index of maximum value, index of minimum value, logical sum (all), logical product (any). These unary operators can be applied in either direction. They can also be applied to produce partial prefix computations. Some details on the patterns in initial database is listed in Fig. D.1.

We indexed the database with three sets of graph invariants derived from the control tree for each pattern. The second set contained all of the first set plus additional invariants. Similarly, the third set contained all of the second set plus additional invariants.

All three sets contained the following invariants:

- number of interior nodes,
- number of leaf nodes,
- number of array references, and

Table D.1
Initial pattern groups

Group Name	Pattern Count	Group Purpose
Dyadic Whole Vector	10	dyadic operators on two entire vectors
Dyadic Whole Matrix	10	dyadic operators on two entire matrices
Dyadic Index Vector	10	dyadic operators on elements of vectors selected by index set
Dyadic Index Matrix	10	dyadic operators on sections of matrices selected by index set
Dyadic Section Vector	10	dyadic operators on cross sections of two vectors
Dyadic Section Matrix	10	dyadic operators on cross sections of two matrices
Dyadic One Matrix	40	dyadic operators on scalar and one row/column of a matrix
Dyadic Section One Matrix	40	dyadic operators on scalar and cross section of matrix row or column
Extend Whole Vector	20	dyadic operator to entire vector and scalar
Extend Whole Matrix	60	dyadic operators on entire matrix and scalar
Extend Section Vector	20	dyadic operators on scalar and cross section of vector
Extend Section Matrix	60	dyadic operators on scalar and cross section of matrix
Binary Whole Vector	5	dot product and related operators on entire vectors
Binary Whole Matrix	15	matrix multiply and related operators on entire matrices
Binary Section Vector	5	dot product and related operators on cross sections of vectors
Unary Whole Vector	26	unary operators on an entire vector
Unary Whole Matrix	52	unary operators on rows or columns of an entire matrix
Unary Section Vector	26	unary operators on a cross section of a vector
Unary Section Matrix	52	unary operators on cross sections of rows or columns of a matrix
Monadic Section	4	monadic operators on cross sections of arrays
Monadic Whole	4	monadic operators on entire arrays
Recur Whole Vector	7	linear recurrences on entire vectors
Star Whole Matrix	12	star patterns on entire matrices
Store Whole Vector	2	assign values to entire vector
Store Whole Matrix	8	assign values to entire matrix
Store Index Vector	2	assign values to elements selected by an index vector
Store Index Matrix	8	assign values to sections selected by an index vector
Store Section Vector	2	assign values to cross section of a vector
Store Section Matrix	8	assign values to cross section of a matrix

- number of scalar variable references.

The second and third sets contained the following additional invariants:

- number of additive operators (addition, subtraction) and
- number of multiplicative operators (multiplication, division).

The third sets contained the following additional invariants:

- number of boolean operators (and, or, etc.),
- number of relational operators (equal, less than, etc.), and
- number of intrinsic operators (such as modulo or, exponentiation).

The first invariant set divided the 536 patterns in 113 groups which had the same index. The distribution of the number of groups with a given number of patterns in that group is listed in Fig. D.2.

Table D.2
Distribution of groups with invariant set 1

Group Size	Number of Groups
1	62
2	19
3	1
4	13
5	1
6	5
7	1
9	6
11	1
12	4
18	3
19	1
20	1
35	1
36	3

The second invariant set divided the 536 patterns in 173 groups which had the same index. The distribution of the number of groups with a given number of patterns in that group is listed in Fig. D.3.

The third invariant set divided the 536 patterns in 213 groups which had the same index. The distribution of the number of groups with a given number of patterns in that group is listed in Fig. D.4.

For our worst-case initial set of patterns, we can limit the number of patterns to be examined to be eight or less by comparing nine integer invariants.

Table D.3
Distribution of groups with invariant set 2

Group Size	Number of Groups
1	95
2	57
3	3
4	25
6	6
7	1
8	9
12	3
13	1
23	1
24	3

Table D.4
Distribution of groups with invariant set 3

Group Size	Number of Groups
1	93
2	97
3	3
4	52
5	1
7	1
8	15

Computational Confluence and Control Group Size

In Chap. 12, we asserted that although the computational confluence heuristic can find, in the worst case, 2^k sets of statements, the actual number of sets is always small in practice. The reason is that the bound k is the number of statements executed under the same flow of control conditions.

In this section, we present some statistics that show that for real programs of the type we are interested in, using the representation that we propose, the number of statements executed under the same flow of control conditions is often quite small.

We analyzed the computational kernels of application codes from the Perfect Club (12), SPEC92 (16), Numerical Recipes (linear algebra algorithms) (41). This collection of code consisted of 45 Fortran source files containing 6,245 lines of non-comment source. While this may seem like a small sample, it is important to note that these are just the subroutines that contributed 80% or more of the CPU time used by the application. They are exactly the subroutines that our profile-driven system would examine. In many of the Perfect Club and SPEC92 codes, there were only one or two subroutines in the computation kernel of the application.

The distribution of the number of groups with a given number of items in a control group is listed in Fig. D.5.

Table D.5
Distribution of control group sizes

Group Size	Number of Groups
2	48
3	34
4	23
5	6
6	14
7	2
8	6
9	6
10	4
11	4
12	1
13	8
14	2
15	2
18	2
19	1
20	1
22	1
23	1
25	1
26	1
28	2
33	1
38	1
51	2
99	1
111	1

This data shows that while the complexity of the computational confluence heuristic is exponential in theory, in practice the size of the set that the heuristic can choose from is often small. 137 out of 170 (80%) of the control groups in our sample have 10 or fewer members. All but 4 of the larger control groups are the root of the control tree. The heuristic won't choose most of the possible subsets of these sets, due to data-flow constraints on the semantics of the extracted subprogram. As a result, the actual performance of the heuristic is quite acceptable.

Besides the inherent character of the computations analyzed, there is also another factor

at work in keeping the size of control groups small. This is the semantic-preserving transformations performed in the pre-processing step. Several of these transformations have
the side effect of reducing the size of control groups. Maximal loop distribution creates
loop nests with the minimum number of statements necessary to preserve semantics. Conditional distribution creates conditional structures with the minimal number of dependent
statements necessary to preserve semantics. Loop rerolling folds multiple assignment statements into single statements by increasing the number of loop iterations. Other traditional
compiler optimizations help to a lesser extent.

References

[1] Aho A.V., Hopcroft J., and Ullman J. D. *The Design and Analysis of Algorithms.* McGraw-Hill, New York, 1974.

[2] Aho A. V., Sethi R., and Ullman J.D. *Compilers: Principles, Techniques, and Tools.* Addison-Wesley, Reading, MA, 1986.

[3] Bhansali S., Hagemeister J.R., et al. Parallelizing Sequential Programs by Algorithm-level Transformations. In *Third Workshop on Program Comprehension* (1994), IEEE Computer Society Press, New York, 100–107.

[4] Bhansali S. and Hagemeister J.R. A Pattern Matching Approach for Reusing Software Libraries in Parallel Systems. In *Proceedings of the Workshop on Knowledge Based Systems for the Reuse of Program Libraries* (1995), Sophia Anthipolis, France.

[5] Biggerstaff T.J. Design Recovery for Maintenance and Reuse. *IEEE Computer 22,*7 (1989), 36–49.

[6] Biggerstaff T.J., Mitbander B.G., and Webster D.E. Program Understanding and the Concept Assignment Problem. *Communications of the ACM 37,*5 (May 1994), 72–82.

[7] Budd T. *An APL Compiler.* Springer-Verlag, New York, 1988.

[8] Chin D. and Quilici A. DECODE: A Cooperative Program Understanding Environment. *Journal of Software Maintenance 8,*1 (1996), to appear.

[9] Cooper K. and Kennedy K. Interprocedural side-effect analysis in linear time. In *Proc. SIGPLAN '88 Conf. on Programming Language and Design* ACM, New York (1988), 247–258.

[10] Cooper K. and Kennedy K. Fast interprocedural alias analysis. In *Conf. Rec. 15th ACM Symposium on Principles of Programming Languages.* ACM, New York (1989), 49–59.

[11] *CXperf User's Guide.* Hewlett-Packard Company, 1998.

[12] Cybenko, G., Kipp, L., Pointer, L., and Kuck, D. Supercomputer Performance Evaluation and the Perfect Benchmarks(tm). In *Proceedings of ICS* (1990), Amsterdam, Netherlands.

[13] DeMarco T. *Structured Analysis and System Specification.* Prentice-Hall, New York, 1979.

[14] DiMartino B. and Iannello G. Towards Automated Code Parallelization through Program Comprehension. In *Third Workshop on Program Comprehension* (1994), IEEE Computer Society Press, New York, 108–115.

[15] DiMartino B. and Iannello G. PAP Recognizer: a Tool for the Automatic Recognition of Parallelizable Patterns. In *Fourth Workshop on Program Comprehension* (1996), IEEE Computer Society Press, New York, 164–173.

[16] Dixit, K. CINT2.0 and CFP2.0 Benchmark Descriptions. *SPEC Newsletter 3,*4 (1991), 18–21.

[17] Dongarra, J.J., Croz, J.D., Hammarling, S., and Hanson, R.J. An extended set of FORTRAN basic linear algebra subprograms. *ACM Trans. on Mathematical Software 14,*1 (March 1988), 1–17.

[18] Ferrante, J., Ottenstein, K.J., and Warren, J.D. The program dependence graph and its use in optimization. *ACM Trans. on Programming Languages and Systems 9,*3 (July 1987), 319–349.

[19] Floyd R. W. and Beigel R. *The Language of Machines: An Introduction to Computability and Formal Languages.* W. H. Freeman and Company, New York (1994).

[20] Graham S.L., Kessler P.B., and M.K. McKusick. gprof: A Call Graph Execution Profiler. In *SIGPLAN '82 Symposium on Compiler Construction* (1982), ACM, New York, 120–126.

[21] Garey R. M. and Johnson D. S. *Computers and Intractability: A guide to the theory of NP-Completeness.* W. H. Freeman and Company, New York (1979).

[22] Harandi M.T. and Ning J.Q. *Knowledge-Based Program Analysis. IEEE Software 7,*1 (1990), 74–81.

[23] Harel D. and Tarjan R. Fast algorithms for finding nearest common ancestor. *SIAM Journal on Computing 13,*2 (1984), 338–355.

[24] Hartman, J. *Automatic control understanding for natural programs.* Ph.D. Thesis, University of Texas at Austin, 1991.

[25] Hausler P.A., Pleszkoch M.G. et al. Using Function Abstraction to Understand Program Behavior. *IEEE Software 7,*1 (1990), 55–63.

[26] Kernighan B. W. and Ritchie D. M. *The C Programming Language.* Prentice Hall, Englewood Cliffs, NJ (1988).

[27]Kessler C.W. and Paul W.J. Automatic parallelization by pattern-matching. In *Parallel Computation, 2nd Intl. ACPC Conference Proceedings* (1994), Springer-Verlag, New York.

[28]Kessler C.W. *Automatische Parallelisierung numerischer Programme durch Mustererkennung.* Ph.D. Thesis, Universitaet Saarbruecken, 1994.

[29]Kessler C.W. Pattern-Driven Automatic Parallelization. *Scientific Programming 5,*3 (1996) 251–274.

[30]Kobler J., Schoning U., and Toran J. *The Graph Isomorphism Problem: Its Structural Complexity.* Birkhauser, Boston (1993).

[31]Kozaczynski V., Ning J., and Engberts A. Program Concept Recognition and Transformation. *IEEE Trans. on Software Engineering 18,*12 (1992) 1065–1074.

[32]Kozaczynski V. and Ning J. Automated Program Understanding by Concept Recognition. *Automated Software Engineering 1,*1 (1994) 61–78.

[33]Lanubile F. and Visaggio G. Function Recovery Based on Program Slicing. In *International Conference on Software Maintenance* (1993), IEEE Computer Society Press, New York, 396–404.

[34]Loeliger J.D., Metzger R.C., Seligman M., and Stroud S. Pointer Target Tracking: An Empirical Study. In *Supercomputing '91* (1991), IEEE Computer Society Press, New York, 14-23.

[35]McConnell R. M. and Spinrad J. Linear-time modular decomposition and efficient transitive orientation of undirected graphs. Technical Report, Dept. of CS, Univ. of Colorado at Boulder, (1993).

[36]Metzger R.C. and Stroud, S. Interprocedural Constant Propagation: An Empirical Study. *ACM Letters on Programming Languages and Systems 2,*1 (March 1993), 213-232.

[37]Mercer R.W. The CONVEX FORTRAN 5.0 Compiler. In *International Supercomputer Conference* (1988).

[38]Muchnick S.S. *Advanced Compiler Design and Implementation.* Morgan Kaufmann, San Francisco, 1997.

[39]Perlis A. and Rugaber S. The APL Idiom List. Yale Univ. Comp. Sci Tech. Report #87, (1977).

[40]Pinter S.S. and Pinter R.Y. Program Optimization and Parallelization Using Idioms. *ACM Trans. on Programming Languages and Systems 16,*3 (1994), 1–21.

[41]Press, W.H., Teuklosky, S.A., Vetterling, W.T., and Flannery, B.P. *Numerical Recipes in Fortran 77* Cambridge University Press, New York, 1996.

[42]Quilici A. and Woods S. Toward a Constraint-Satisfaction Framework for Evaluating Program-Understanding Algorithms. In *Fourth Workshop on Program Comprehension* (1996), IEEE Computer Society Press, New York, 55–64.

[43]Quilici A. A Memory-Based Approach to Recognizing Programming Plans. *Communications of the ACM 37,*5 (1994), 84–93.

[44]Quilici A. A Hybrid Approach to Recognizing Programming Plans. In *Working Conference on Reverse Engineering* (1993), IEEE Computer Society Press, New York, 126–133.

[45]Read R. C. and Corneil D. G. The graph isomorphism disease. *Journal of Graph Theory. 1,*4 (1977), 339–363.

[46]Rich C. and Waters R. *The Programmer's Apprentice.* ACM Press, New York (1990).

[47]Snyder L. Recognition and Selection of Idioms for Code Optimization. *Acta Informatica 17,*3 (1982) 327–348.

[48]Tarjan R. E. Depth first search and linear graph algorithms. *SIAM Journal on Computing 1,*2 (1972), 146–160.

[49]Tremblay J. and Sorenson P. G. *The Theory and Practice of Compiler Writing.* McGraw-Hill, New York (1985).

[50]Weiser M. Program Slicing. *IEEE Trans. on Software Engineering 10,*4 (1984), 352–357.

[51]Wen Z. New algorithms for the LCA problem and the binary tree reconstruction problem. *Information Processing Letters 51,*1 (1994) 11–16.

[52]Wills L. *Automated Program Recognition by Graph Parsing.* Ph.D Thesis, A.I. Technical Report 1358, MIT Artificial Intelligence Lab (1992).

[53] Wills L. Flexible control for program recognition. In *Working Conference on Reverse Engineering* (1993), IEEE Computer Society Press, New York 134–143.

[54] Wolfe M. *High Performance Compilers for Parallel Computing*. Addison-Wesley, Reading, MA, 1996.

[55] Woods S. and Yang Q. The Program Understanding Problem: Analysis and a Heuristic Approach. In *18th International Conference on Software Engineering* (1996), IEEE Computer Society Press, New York 6–15.

[56] Woods S. and Yang Q. Program Understanding as Constraint Satisfaction: Representation and Reasoning Techniques. *Automated Software Engineering 1*,1 (1998) 247–181.

[57] Woods, S., Quilici, A.E., and Yang, Q. *Constraint-Based Design Recovery for Software Engineering*. Kluwer Academic Publishers, Boston, 1998.

[58] Zima H. and Chapman B. *Supercompilers for Parallel and Vector Computers*. ACM Press, New York (1990).

[59] Zima H. and Chapman B. Compiling for Distributed-Memory Systems. *Proceedings of the IEEE 81*,2 (February 1993), 264–287.

Index